This book is a tribute to great Swiss companies that have stood the test of time. Looking over this collection of texts, it is clear that the success of these businesses – down the generations and across our borders – is based on a number of common denominators. First of all comes tradition, of course: authentic expertise and formulas handed down from one generation to the next and shrouded in secrecy.

And then there is innovation. Contrary to popular belief, Switzerland is a hotbed of creativity! Whether in terms of innovative products, communication, distribution or entire business models, Swiss firms lead the way on all fronts. And like great leaders everywhere, they are also models of perseverance.

Their vision is fixed on the long-term. The success stories captured in this work are underpinned by a number of key principles: the need to remain true to ideals, build a reputation and produce the very highest quality, above and beyond the lure of mere profitability. Behind these brands – no matter how diverse their sectors – stand generations of men and women with the utmost respect for their workforce and for investment in the tools of production. Quality is their gold standard. But beyond their business background, they also share a robust ethic which they uphold both within their companies and often within the region at large – that of "Swissness".

In their bid to create long-term jobs and to perpetuate expertise and sustainable development, the country's great companies are Swiss not only in name but also in their values. Values that can of course have a very positive effect on the economy.

In an era dominated by a fixation with short-term profits, the strength of the entrepreneurial principles and long-term vision of the great Swiss companies is the exception that proves the rule. "The Little Book of Big Swiss Houses" is a joyous testament to this.

Jean-Philippe Zérafa   Tiffany Büsser

Interviews

FAVARGER / Vesna Zuvela, CEO

What was your first contact with the brand?

A friend gave me a box of Avelines. It was the best chocolate I had ever tasted. At the time it didn't cross my mind that I would work for Favarger one day. I was involved in Strategy and Product Development from 2009 and officially appointed CEO in 2013.

Looking back almost 200 years, what have been the most significant developments of Favarger?

A major turning point in Favarger's history came after the First World War with the launch of two products which have since become the brand's signatures: the legendary Aveline which launched in 1922 and the equally famous Nougaline first sold in 1932. Favarger began producing couverture chocolate for confectioners and for local producers to cover "biscuits" in 1956. This was another milestone for the company as it saw a significant increase in production. Favarger chocolate's signature flavour became more and more widespread. In 2010, we repositioned the Favarger brand in the super-premium sector by upgrading the already high quality of the products to make them unique on the market. Our goal was to produce only 100% natural chocolates across the board: from Aveline to fresh chocolates.

What is your biggest challenge nowadays ?

Consumers are becoming increasingly demanding and are constantly searching for new products. Our role is to innovate and use our skills to meet consumer needs. We are constantly looking for new flavours and new packaging. Our challenge nowadays is to establish ourselves in new markets where there's demand for high quality chocolate and in which Favarger's legacy and expertise are major assets. In addition to Europe, we now distribute our chocolates throughout the Asian and American markets

How do you see the brand in 10 years?

In 10 years I see Favarger as a strong and successful brand available throughout the marketplace which continues to innovate, inspire and indulge chocolate lovers all over the world. We will achieve our goals by staying true to our expertise and traditional production to always guarantee the highest quality of our chocolates.

ZIMMERLI OF SWITZERLAND / Marcel Hossli, CEO

What was your first contact with the brand?

I clearly remember reading an article about Zimmerli, its Swiss production and its many celebrity clients in a business magazine. That must have been about 15 years ago. When I heard in 2008 that Zimmerli was looking for a new CEO, it was immediately obvious to me that this would be my dream job. Fortunately, they chose me. My high expectations have since been fully met.

What is your biggest challenge nowadays ?

Zimmerli of Switzerland manufactures the world's finest and most beautiful underwear. And all by hand in Switzerland. This is both a commitment and a challenge, because production in Switzerland is much more expensive than it is abroad, for example in Asia. We are nevertheless convinced that this apparent drawback represents an essential advantage for us and our customers. Our production unit only employs people who have devoted their great expertise to the proverbial 'Zimmerli quality' for years, even decades. And the proximity of the production gives us great flexibility and speed.

How do you see the brand in 10 years ?

At the core and the mission of Zimmerli, not much will have changed. Even a decade into the future, our products will not

1. Carl Elsener, Victorinox, CEO.

2. Alain Zimmermann, Baume & Mercier, CEO.

3. Didier Guillon, Valmont, CEO.

4. Vesna Zuvela, Favarger, CEO.

5. Marcel Hossli, Zimmerli of Switzerland, CEO.

be for the mass market, but for those people who appreciate true, honest quality. We will remain faithful to our commitment to have "The world's finest underwear – handmade in Switzerland since 1871", and to processing the very highest quality natural fibres in our Swiss Manufacture. However, what is certain is that Zimmerli will have continued to grow in popularity and notoriety. We will continue to work very hard on that, now and into the future.

BAUME ET MERCIER / Alain Zimmermann, CEO

What was your first contact with the brand?

That was actually through a Hampton, with a white dial and an amazing "racing green" strap I bought in 1996! I loved that watch at first sight and have been really proud of wearing it! I still keep this watch which reminds me a great time.

What is your biggest challenge nowadays ?

To perpetuate the motto defined by our founders and which is clearly the driving force behind the success of our Maison: "Accept only perfection. Only manufacture watches of the highest quality". That's a challenge but also a fantastic philosophy, creating quality at an affordable price.

How do you see the brand in 10 years?

A brand established internationally and that remains loyal to our positioning: high-quality watches for both men and women, with a timeless and elegant design at an affordable price, and with a single purpose: to be THE watch partner to mark the most memorable moments in lives.

VALMONT / Didier Guillon, CEO

How do you see the brand in 10 years ?

We built this brand around a number of strategic choices, based on changes in the world of distribution. Rather than creating an attractive product for the sole benefit of the mainstream perfume industry dominated by the multi-brand giants, we opted to work with chains such as Amavita, which offer an exclusive service and expert guidance alongside their perfume products. And

then about a decade ago we entered the spa sector. Our distribution must remain highly selective, making more use of large department stores, as this gives our brand much greater visibility. We are starting to sell at Saks in the USA, Holt Renfrew in Canada.

Where will your next spas be located ?

We've received a large number of inquiries, and we need to be mindful of the energy required to achieve the impeccable results our image demands. We are currently working on projects with some of the world's finest hotels, in L'Auberge du Jeu de Paume in Chantilly, at the Château de la Messardière in St Tropez and in the Maldives, as well as the Crans-Ambassador in Switzerland.

VICTORINOX / Carl Elsener, CEO

What role does the family play in a business like yours?

The management of Victorinox has been handed down over four generations. Family values have had a major impact on our corporate values. My grandfather and father always had a long-term vision. The key is not to be driven by a short-term vision or by pressure from shareholders. That's one of the strengths of a family business.

I learnt from my father that if a company wants to enjoy long-term success, it must concentrate on three things: its staff, its clients and its products. If you invest energy in these areas, you clearly multiply your chances of success. We do everything to help our staff work with enthusiasm and interest, which leads to quality products and satisfied clients. (Editor's note: we did indeed come across many smiling faces in the corridors.)

Our company is based on mutual trust, with 900 staff at the head office. They know that we can't promise jobs for life, but they also know that we'll do our utmost with that in mind. After 9/11, sales of Swiss knives plummeted by 30%. It was that very trust that helped us weather the storm. We were really up against it but we managed to hold on to all our staff.

Humility is another core family and corporate value. It has

always been clear to us that our success is due to the collective efforts of all our staff and not to a tiny group at the apex of the pyramid. As a manager, if you are mindful of the people to whom you owe your success, your ego and your bonuses are unlikely to grow too big.

How can you keep on going and continue to innovate after 130 years?

You have to make sure you're open to everything: new trends, new client needs, internal needs. Victorinox has always been a listening company. Both directly and indirectly, we hear what our partners and subsidiaries have to say and try to act on that. In the digital age, Swiss knives are authentic in their tangible worth. And that's rare! When you give your child their first Swiss knife, you see a timeless spark in their eyes. Just the same as it was 30 or 40 years ago. We offer courses to schools and clubs, where children are taught the many ways to use Swiss knives safely. They love it! It makes a change from tablets and games consoles, and parents appreciate that too.

What does the concept of Swiss-made have to offer in the face of Chinese competition?

The reasons for the success of the Swiss economy and its ability to withstand competition from China no doubt include our long-term vision and our focus on quality.

Our training system is also a tremendous asset – the future of Switzerland is in the hands of its young apprentices – true professionals who take pride in what they do. Their drive and commitment underpin our national success. Our people are skilled, gifted and passionate about their work. In fact, quality and practicality are hardwired into our system.

What are the challenges for a brand like Victorinox?

We are a Swiss company based on products for which quality and practicality are essential hallmarks. The majority of our products are made here in Switzerland, and given that our focus is on the rest of the world – 90% of the total knife production is exported – our greatest challenge is the strength of the Swiss franc. We have to keep a close eye on quality and constantly improve our production.

Another challenge is to maintain consistency, despite the diversification of our company. The Swiss Army Knife is our core product, but over the years we have also branched into watches, in 1989, in 1999 into travel gear, 2001 into clothes and in 2007 into fragrances. We have to make sure that these different categories are seen by clients as belonging to one and the same brand. To this end, our divisions are working hand-in-hand in the development of new products.

How do you see the future of the company, the "fifth-generation"? What are the key skills required to keep the flag flying?

For our family, the key objective is to ensure that the values on which the success of Victorinox has been based for generations are passed on. Of course, we hope to keep things within the family. To my mind, managing Victorinox is about being open-minded and setting an example. When we require certain things of our staff, we have to be able to lead the way. You have to love people. That's the only way to understand them and hear what it is your customers want. On top of that, you have to be able to surround yourself with people whose skills complement yours and strive to make sure that everyone works together in an effective and successful manner.

Summary

BALLY

Legendary shoemakers

Bally is first and foremost a family affair. The brand started in Schönenwerd, a small, quiet hamlet in north-west Switzerland, making elastic ribbons. However, a trip to Paris changed the company's fate forever. While on a business trip, Carl Franz Bally decided to buy his wife a gift: some lace-up ankle boots which were very fashionable at the time. Unable to remember her size, Carl Franz bought a dozen pairs in all sizes, and was sure that one of them would fit. While visiting the Parisian factory that made the boots, he noticed that every pair had elastic button clasps similar to those made by his family in Switzerland. Inspired by his discovery, he decided to extend the company's activity to include making shoes. From then on, with the help of designers, he and his brother Fritz began manually producing leather shoes in Carl Franz's cellar. They did not suspect then that they were laying the foundation for what was to be one of the first global luxury brands. The Bally Company was founded in Schönenwerd in 1851. Three years later, the first factory was built in the heart of the village. When Fritz retired in 1854, the company changed its name to CF Bally, later becoming CF Bally and sons when the founder handed the reins to his children in 1892. By the time of his death in 1899, the company had created 3,000 jobs, and was producing two million pairs of shoes per year. The pioneering spirit was in the family genes. Although Edward Bally

LEGENDARY ACHIEVEMENT: STANDING ON TOP OF THE WORLD

In the 1950s when Bally captivated an urban, elegant and sporty clientèle and supplied the Olympic team, the brand reached even more remarkable heights. In the immaculate, virgin snow, two mountaineers succeeded in climbing Mount Everest while wearing Reindeer-Himalaya Bally boots, developed based on the brand's mountain boots. Sir Edmund Hillary and Sherpa Tenzing Norgay reached the top of the world, at the same time proving the company's exceptional expertise in creating high-technical performance shoes.

had already been travelling the world for a decade, he supervised the openings of the first international boutiques in Geneva and Montevideo- Uruguay in 1870. International growth would continue steadily with boutiques in Buenos Aires, Paris and London in 1873, 1879 and 1882 respectively. Purchasing a building on the Bahnhofstrasse in Zurich in 1927 was equally ambitious.Throughout the 20th century the brand opened numerous boutiques. Its international expansion took off again in the 1980s and 1990s with the advent of major new markets, such as Asia and North America. 163 years later Bally represents Swiss heritage using the finest materials, with elegance and great attention to detail. It is renowned for its modernist approach and innovation, as much as for its timelessness and functionality.

TIMELESS BALLY ICONS

The company combines a forward-thinking mix of ancestral artisan techniques and cutting-edge technology, to create high-quality leather goods. Over two centuries, Bally's creativity has transformed it into an empire with an international reputation. The brand's ever-classic styles prove that a shoe with perfect functionality can evolve without ever disappearing. Scribe, Bally stripes, Zurich pumps and leather accessories, are all part of Bally's living heritage of design. Created for the brand's centenary in 1951, the men's shoe "Scribe" is the essence of Bally's tradition of quality. Even today, this item requires over 200 production stages and 6 hours of expert artisan work. It is reinvented for 2015 as the elegant Scribe Novo, endowed with a record-breakingly light Goodyear sole. Created in 1939 as a decoration for a woman's shoe, the "Bally stripe" motif is a timeless homage to the Swiss flag. Inspired by the visual effect of the movement of a train in the flag's colours, it is a testament to the brand's origins and remains its hallmark. The first Bally pump was a feminine revolution when it was created in 1890. The iconic "Zurich" has since been a symbol of tradition and elegance. The collection now includes a large choice of shapes, colours, materials, and heel heights. In 1956, the brand's alpine roots elevated its design to an iconic status: the "Curling" boot was born, created for the Swiss Winter Olympics team in Cortina D'Ampezzo. This highly technical shoe was perfectly adapted to outdoor winter sports. In particular, it was equipped with a water-resistant sole to ensure comfort and durability.

Now, other creations have established themselves as points of reference:

The **Moritz** collection symbolises Bally's continued quest to create beautiful, modern luggage that is also timeless.

The **Papillon** collection combines the brand's pioneering techniques in leather work with great functionality, and respects the highest luxury standards.

The **Corner** bag is inspired by the gentleman's corner of a man's shoe and is available in small or medium sizes in a range of exotic finishes.

ART, DESIGN AND ARCHITECTURE

Whether it be for use in its own premises, for inspiring a collection or in its non-commercial activities, Bally has always celebrated architecture and design. Architecture has been an important backdrop for its activities since the first premises were built in Schönenwerd in 1865. Thereafter in 1919 The Bally Kosthaus- a dedicated employee complex, also in Schönenwerd, was designed by the famous modernist architect Karl Moser Later, the majestic National Congress of Brazil building, created by Oscar Niemeyer, featured as the star of a men's campaign. When Andrée Putman renovated Capitole (Zurich) in 1995, she also put her talent to redesigning the interiors of the legendary Bally boutiques in Geneva and Zurich. In the late 1990s, the brand drew inspiration from the famous "Panton S chair" by Verner Panton for the curves of its women's shoes. To celebrate its 160th birthday, Bally is partnering with Herman Miller for a charity project— its emblematic stripes will feature on the famous Eames chairs, in a limited edition series. Pursuing the collaboration with famous designers and architects inspired by the modernist movement, Bally' s emblematic flagship in London has been designed by Sir David Chipperfield.

Enhancing both its place within the world of luxury and its modernist roots, the Swiss shoemaker and leather goods merchant presented its new design collection at the Art Basel salon in 2014. The collection included furniture by modernists Pierre Jeanneret and Jean Prouvé alongside a unique piece by duo Kolkoz. The project is a work-in-progress which will continue at Art Basel, Miami and Shanghai. A travelling exhibition dedicated to the values which captivate Bally: modernity, function, and innovation.

BAUME & MERCIER

Bringing watchmaking heritage to life

Clifton 1830 model is the cornerstone of the collection, loosely based on the historic instrument owned by the Baume & Mercier museum.

The story began in 1830, when Louis-Victor and Célestin Baume founded a watch dealership called "Frères Baume" in Les Bois in the Swiss Jura. The two entrepreneurs rapidly grew the family business, making quality watches equipped with the technological innovations of their time. Aware as they were of the importance of finding outlets beyond Jura's mountains, they set out early on to conquer the world. Pioneering Célestin Baume founded a branch in London as early as 1851. Its activity rapidly expanded, and the House won a solid international reputation. In 1876, Louis-Victor Baume's two sons took over the family business. Alcide lived in Switzerland to monitor and follow up production. Arthur took charge of the House's international standing. He went to Philadelphia, USA, where he opened a branch in 1876. The House of Frères Baume also attended the Great International Exhibitions, winning prizes and medals. With the arrival of the third generation, the globally renowned House took a new direction. In 1919, the young William Baume took advantage of the jubilant atmosphere following the First World War and partnered with Paul Mercier, a colourful character who was an art-lover and a shrewd businessman. The two men then created Baume & Mercier which, subsequently established in Geneva, became a fully-fledged manufacture. They received the prestigious "Poinçon de Genève" for

the excellence of their timepieces. By 1924, the brand was one of the largest Genevan watchmaking manufactures. Baume & Mercier joined the luxury group which would become Richemont at the end of the 1980s, gaining a new lease of life. The company is present in over 100 countries via a selective network of 1,600 retail outlets, a large number of which are in Asia, the UAE, France and the USA, and today it employs just over 200 people. After almost two centuries in existence, the Swiss watchmaking House is among the oldest watchmaking brands still operating, and has created an image which evokes elegance and accessible luxury.

AN INTERNATIONAL PRIZE LIST

Thanks to its time measuring instruments, "Frères Baume" won ten Grand Prix awards and seven gold medals at international exhibitions and shows in Paris, Melbourne, Zurich, Amsterdam, London and Chicago. As well as being beautiful and complex, Baume & Mercier watches have a rare degree of precision. They set accuracy records and have won various timekeeping competitions, in particular the precision timing trials held by the Kew Observatory near London. Later, the Galaxie and Stardust models won the Golden Rose at the international Baden-Baden competition in Germany, between 1972 and 1973, this time for their design.

SWISS-MADE EXCELLENCE

Since it was founded, the company has made its pieces using "établissage", an ancestral technique where the components made according to the designs provided by the brand are assembled in their workshops in the Swiss Jura, in particular in Les Brenets. Each piece, after being carefully inspected, is assembled in a workshop with a controlled atmosphere. Each detail complies with the rigorous standards put in place by the founding family in 1830: from the totality of a bracelet to the watertightness of a case, from correct functioning of each complication to respecting strict precision criteria.

AN ETERNAL PROMISE

Baume & Mercier continue to honour the promise its founders made almost 200 years ago: "Accept only perfection, only manufacture watches of the highest quality". The House

184 YEARS OF WATCHMAKING EXPERTISE

1830 The "Frères Baume" House opened its first watch dealership in Les Bois in the Swiss Jura.

1851 The "Baume Brothers" branch was founded in London.

1852 "Baume Brothers" was set up in Australia.

1892 "Baume Brothers" won the Kew Observatory precision timing competition.

1918 Paul Mercier partnered with William Baume. Together, they created the Baume & Mercier House in Geneva.

1919 Baume & Mercier movements were awarded the "Poinçon de Genève" hallmark, the highest watchmaking craftsmanship distinction.

1950's They acquired a new production system (chronograph movements) with the C.H. manufacture Meylan Watch.

1964 Baume & Mercier chose the Greek letter Phi as their new visual emblem, the golden number of Antiquity representing perfect proportions.

1973 The sumptuous "Stardust" model won the Golden Rose of the International Baden-Baden competition in Düsseldorf.

2002 Baume & Mercier opened its own watchmaking workshops in Les Brenets in the Swiss Jura.

2013 The Clifton collection for men was launched internationally.

2014 Lancement international de la collection féminine Promesse.

Capeland 10006,
Chronographe Flyback.

Hampton 10033.

places great importance on restoring all watches it has made in the past, as, in keeping with the brand's philosophy, there isn't a single Baume & Mercier watch which cannot be repaired. The artisan-watchmakers' skills are particularly varied, and some of them are tasked with repairing old Baume & Mercier watches. The emotion contained in a watch is priceless, and so everything is done to bring them back to life, whatever their age or state.

EMBLEMATIC PIECES AND COLLECTIONS

The Promesse collection is intensely delicate and timeless. A classic, precious watch conveying a strong emotional charge, Promesse draws its inspiration from almost 100 years of history of feminity and seduction. A true ode to femininity, its light design includes an oval bezel curled up in a soft, round case.

The Linea collection, created in 1987, recalls a completely feminine balance with its fluid and original lines. This free and contemporary reinterpretation of a 1950s model offers, thanks to an ingenious interchangeable bracelets system, the possibility of adapting the watch to one's outfit of the moment.

The Clifton collection is the expertise inherited from Baume & Mercier incarnate. Inspired by a watch launched in the 1950s, it includes different finishes and complications (simple watch, GMT, complete calendar and chronograph). The Clifton 1830 model is the cornerstone of the collection, loosely based on the historic instrument owned by the Baume & Mercier museum. It has a manually wound calibre with a double barrel, offering a 90-hour power reserve.

The Capeland chronograph is part of a "sport-chic" line, with its vintage design inspired by a chronograph single push-piece model from 1948. These chronographs created for adventure present two measuring scales (tachymeter and telemeter).

The Hampton collection for men and women is both chic and timeless, with a rectangular case inspired by a model launched during the Art Deco period (1930s-1940s). The collection's emblematic piece is animated by a rectangular mechanical hand-wound calibre, specially made for Baume & Mercier by La Joux-Perret.

With **the Classima collection**, Baume & Mercier go to the heart of the matter by choosing fineness. Drawing its inspiration from an extra-slim grey gold automatic watch from 1965, Classima is marked by fineness and purity.

Promesse 10165-10166.

GENEVE

PATEK PHILIPPE

Generation after Generation

Since it was created on May 1st 1839, Patek Philippe has endeavoured to perpetuate the tradition of exceptional watchmaking. After 175 years of uninterrupted business, the company now has 55 movements and produces around 55,000 watches per year, sold through 441 points of sale in 67 countries. It is the last family-run independent manufacturer in Geneva and benefits from a total creative freedom to design, produce and assemble watches that specialists rank amongst the best in the world. Its watches regularly send auction prices through the roof, selling for several million francs. In a sale that set a world record, the highly complex "Henry Graves" pocket watch (1933) sold for 17 millions CHF.

BIRTH OF AN EXCEPTIONAL MANUFACTURER

When he arrived in Geneva after having been exiled from Poland by Russian forces, Antoine Norbert de Patek became fascinated by the art of watchmaking and the expertise of all the engravers, enamellers and jewellers involved. In 1839, he founded his first watchmaking business and it became an instant success. But he didn't meet his perfect partner, Jean Adrien Philippe, until a few years later. Born in central France, Philippe learnt his trade from his watchmaker father. After his journeyman years, he

Left: the historical building of Patek Philippe & Co (1855) Grand Quai view.
Right: the historical building, today one of the Patek Philippe Salons, Rue de Rhône 41.

Top : Antoine Norbert de Patek's pocket watch (1842). On display at the Patek Philippe Museum (P-01).

Right page : Various historical patents filed by Patek Philippe. Today, the Manufacture counts over 100 patents to its name. Every Patek Philippe watch case is finished by hand. Here, the setting. The third and fourth generations of the Stern family. Mr Philippe Stern and Mr Thierry Stern, respectively.

settled in Paris, where he invented the system for winding and setting a watch using a crown (rather than a key), still in use today. He presented his creations in 1844 at the French Industrial Fair in Paris, where he attracted Patek's attention. Patek convinced Philippe to visit him in Geneva, where the two men agreed on a partnership. Together Patek, an astute businessman, and Philippe, a talented watchmaker, soon formed "Patek, Philippe & Co.". As technical director, Philippe introduced modern production methods, oversaw the manufacture of current models and was constantly optimising manufacturing processes, as well as developing new watches and mechanisms. Patek adopted an innovative marketing style that would see the company's watches become amongst the most sought-after in the world. By participating in the world fairs in Paris and London and gaining fame at other international fairs, they not only became known around the world, but also excellent ambassadors for Geneva. When the partners died and some of their beneficiaries renounced their inheritance, the owners decided to opt for the modern "public company" business type in 1901 and the company became the "Ancienne Manufacture d'horlogerie Patek, Philippe & Cie, Société Anonyme". In 1932, following financial difficulties resulting from the global crisis, the company had to find a buyer. To avoid being bought out by a competitor or liquidated, the management called upon the Stern brothers, one of Patek Philippe's suppliers who owned a watch dial company manufacturer. The two firms were on good terms and the Stern ended up buying the company in its entirety. Henri Stern (1911-2002), Charles Stern's 23 year-old son, joined the company. In 1946, he founded and later became president of the Henri Stern Watch Agency in New York, the sole distributor of Patek Philippe watches in the US. His son Philippe began working at the agency, before joining Patek Philippe Geneva

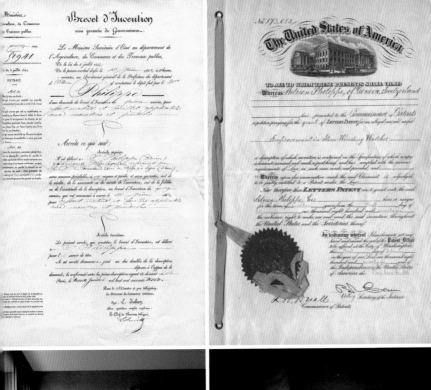

KEY DATES

1839 Patek & Czapek is founded in Geneva.

1844 Jean Adrien Philippe invents a mechanism for pocket watches to be wound and set without a key.

1851 At the Great Exhibition at Crystal Palace in London, the watchmaker has the honour of counting Queen Victoria amongst its customers.

1868 Creation of the first Swiss bracelet watch: a bracelet watch for women wound with a key.

1902 Patek Philippe patents a double chronograph.

1933 Brothers Charles and Jean Stern acquire the "Ancienne Manufacture d'horlogerie Patek, Philippe & Cie".

1946 Henri Stern, son of Charles Stern, reinvigorates the American market by founding "Henri Stern Watch Agency" in NYC. One of the company's movements sets the record for precision for a mechanical watch at the Geneva Observatory, a record still unbroken to this day (1962).

1962 One of the company's movements sets the record for precision for a mechanical watch at the Geneva Observatory, a record still unbroken to this day.

1968 Launch of the Ellipse d'Or Collection of bracelet watches (ref. 3548), with case proportions are inspired by the "golden number".

1976 The Nautilus is launched.

1989 Patek Philippe unveils the Calibre 89 pocket watch, which remains to this day the most complicated portable timepiece in the world (33 complications).

2001 Inauguration of the Patek Philippe Museum.

2009 As the fourth generation of Sterns, Thierry Stern succeeds his father as president of Patek Philippe. The "Patek Philippe Seal" is launched.

2014 Patek Philippe celebrates its 175th anniversary.

Reference 5304R
Grand Complication.
Minute repeater with retrograde
date perpetual calendar

in 1966, where he was charged with developing a new watch model. Philippe was a keen sportsman and a formidable competitor at sailing regattas, inspiring him to create the Nautilus. This elegant sports watch is a masterpiece that has become legendary and highly sought-after. He was appointed managing director in 1977. In the 1980's, he employed a combination of visionary marketing, an entrepreneurial spirit, aesthetic appeal and artistic culture. By hiring watchmaking engineers to turn a manufacturer with a strong emphasis on craftsmanship into an industrial manufacturer, he wanted to guarantee the reproducibility and quality of the components, as well as the long-term maintenance and repair of the watches. An ambitious strategy that paid off for the 150th anniversary of the manufacturer, when the most complicated portable timepiece in the world (the Calibre 89) was developed. The fourth generation of the Stern family, Thierry, joined the manufacturer in 1994 and took over the role of president from his father in 2009. Shortly after his appointment, Patek Philippe launched the Patek Philippe Seal, a mark of excellence. Today, Patek Philippe has become one of the largest independent, family-run manufacturers, with nearly 2,000 employees. The company upholds a tradition of innovation with a considerable repertoire of more than 100 patents. In October 2014 the company celebrates its 175th anniversary.

A SEAL OF EXCELLENCE

The seal of quality was established in 2009. It is the most exacting standard in the whole watchmaking industry and adheres to its founders' vision. The seal applies to the whole watch - such as the perfect combination of a movement and its casing - and includes the development specifications, the manufacture of the movement, the case and all of the casing, as well as the customer service, and any maintenance or repair. It is also the only watchmaking quality stamp to guarantee the maintenance of all the manufacturer's timepieces for their entire life spans, regardless of when they were made.

A FINE WATCHMAKING MUSEUM

Henri Stern had a passion for rare watches that reflected all the expertise that has long been associated with watchmaking. He passed on this passion for rare handcrafts to his son Philippe, who dedicated himself with even more passion for this art. In 2001, he inaugurated the Patek Philippe Museum in the Plainpalais area of Geneva in order to exhibit his treasures: a collection of more than 2,000 watches, automatons and minia-ture enamel paintings, illustrating five centuries of watchmaking history; a selection of masterpieces created in the manufacturer's workshop; and a library of more than 8,000 works dedicated to watchmaking, astronomy and measuring time.

Self-winding movement with
mini-rotor and annual calendar.
Caliber 31-260 REG QA,
with the Patek Philippe Seal.

CARAN D'ACHE

Maison de Haute Écriture

Haran d'Ache, successor to an inestimable expertise, has been creating the very best in writing implements since 1915. Recognised the world over for the excellence and quality of its writing implements and colours, Caran d'Ache combines skilfulness with beauty. A personal item, a technological wonder... Each creation is entirely manufactured in Geneva in the great Swiss tradition, consolidating the precision, passion and the proficiency of specialists in more than ninety fields. This «Swiss-made» excellence is also present in the company's cherished social and ecological values. More than just a brand: a constant companion, a confidant, a source of wonderment... Combining the best from the past and present, Caran d'Ache continues to make its mark today, true to its traditions.

HISTORY AND TRADITION

Originating as La Fabrique Genevoise de Crayons in 1915, Caran d'Ache took on its present name in 1924 when Arnold Schweitzer became head of the company. He renamed it after the pen name of the famous French caricaturist Emmanuel Poiré. The artist, considered one of the founding fathers of the comic strip, signs his work « Caran d'Ache », a transliteration of the Russian word *karandash*, which means pencil.

EXPERTISE

Like the act of writing itself, Caran d'Ache
implements reflect panache, style and heritage.
They are the crystallisation of manufacturing
expertise and well-kept trade secrets passed
down from generation to generation. While the
workshop is fitted out with cutting-edge machines,
the human touch remains essential, and the most
crucial steps of creation can only be carried out
by people. The act of drawing out pen nibs is a
perfect example of a centuries-old technique :
the nib material stretches out to infinity in a rapid
flow until it is cut to form a nib. Only the true
craftsman can spot an erroneous diameter and
adjust the movement to the momentum.

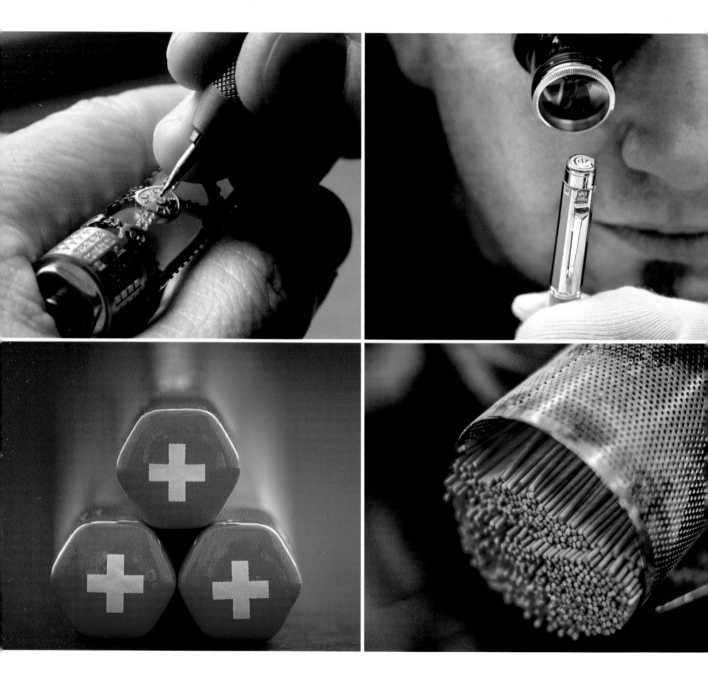

Caran d'Ache is a self-sufficient manufacturer. All its products are entirely designed, developed and produced in Geneva. The company still continues to uphold and develop its centuries-old expertise. Since it was created, the brand has been exploring all types of writing implements in various fields of expression. Coloured pencils, wax pastels, exceptional pieces, exclusive ink: these tools become an extension of the hand in its creative gesture. Caran d'Ache is the world's only manufacturer to produce a full palette of implements for both fine arts and writing in one place. Its creations reveal the incredible artistic liberty that has always flourished at the heart of the Geneva workshops. The company has a distinctly family-like character, and it considers its human capital one of its principal resources. Carole Hubscher, representing the fourth generation in the family line, is at the head of Caran d'Ache today. The creations of the Geneva-based manufacturer are available in more than ninety countries through subsidiaries and distributors, and in three exclusive brand boutiques in Switzerland, Geneva and Zurich.

ALCHEMY

Caran d'Ache plies its alchemy through the enchanting prism of more than three hundred shades. While our colour experts utilise equipment at the forefront of technological innovation, they remain craftsmen who also use their instincts. These material connoisseurs subtly adjust their blends until they obtain the new shade they are seeking. A symphony of colours flows through the full array of media - pencil graphites, markers, pastels, gouaches, inks, watercolours and acrylics - for brilliant results and an excellent resistance to light. Each colour of a given collection must guarantee the same sensation in the stroke, although each is composed of different pigments. The pigments are at the heart of the product, providing depth, opacity and resistance to light.

Ideas take shape within the laboratory, where chemical engineers work uncompromisingly to find the perfect colour. A new colour requires the development of an original formula. Each pigment requires its own unique process. Each one will react differently according to its characteristics. This continuing search for high-quality, long-lasting colours is a daily challenge, making use of the secrets of our manufacturing processes.

Top left, the setting of writing instruments.
Top right, quality control.
Bottom left, Swiss Wood Caran d'Ache pencils made from Swiss wood.
Bottom right, the creation of pencil leads.

OFFICE

Streamlined, ergonomic, made of resistant, enduring
materials and featuring long-lasting cartridges: these
exceptional attributes make the very best in writing
accessible to everyone for day-to-day use.
The reliable, durable products of the «Office» range
are designed to satisfy the needs of the workplace.
Many of these models are vanguard and feature
original designs. Both classic and trendsetting, these
implements offer their users an uncompromising
practicality. Today they have become cult items.
Among the icons of the Office line, the styles of
Fixpencil and Collection 849 have become a tradition.

PERSONALISATION

Take a moment to record an unforgettable moment
iwith a gesture that leaves a lasting memory...
The variations possible through personalising the
colour of Caran d'Ache writing instruments and cases
are as diverse as fingerprints.

INNOVATION AND CREATIVITY

Caran d'Ache creations, unparalleled in terms of materials and technology, originate in one of two in-house R&D departments: colour or writing. These departments were the launchpads of a number of patented inventions that revolutionised drawing and writing, such as Fixpencil and Neocolor. To achieve such accomplishments, the manufacturer has always combined craftsmanship with technological innovation, an alchemy that never fails to produce extraordinary quality.

GOLDSMITH OF EXCEPTIONAL OBJECTS

Coat of mail, wood, precious stones, ceramic... Marvels of craftsmanship with inspired lines, Caran d'Ache Haute Ecriture implements embody a passion for beautiful workmanship. The company's guilloche engravers, lacquerers and polishers make use of historical techniques and objects to ennoble the writing implement. Centuries-old techniques, such as engraving, guilloching, polishing, lacquering and stone setting, impart character to these objects. Each process is meticulously hand-rendered, bringing the object to life.

GUARANTEED FOR LIFE !

With its self-contained expertise, the manufacturer upholds important values such as durability, quality and trustworthiness. This is undoubtedly why its writing instruments are themselves handed down from generation to generation, persisting indelibly through the years. Their lifetime guarantee is the most tangible expression of the philosophy connected to them.

SUSTAINABLE DEVELOPMENT

An everyday commitment, a social responsibility. The quality of Caran d'Ache products is present in the sustainable development of every production stage and in the company's values. All the pencils with FCS or PEFC certifications are guaranteed to be made with wood from protected forests. Caran d'Ache is also a pioneer in the development of a water-based varnish that has allowed for the drastic reduction in its use of solvents. Borrowing from nature's virtues while ensuring its protection, taking inspiration from tradition while upholding craftsmanship : these are the foundations of the company, one that is committed to protecting the environment and human values.

VALMONT

A Swiss elixir for body and mind

Built in 1905, in the stunning, exclusive surroundings above Montreux and the banks of Lake Geneva, the Clinique Valmont was the first in the country dedicated to health and well-being. The clinic provided dietary advice and hydrotherapy sessions. Rainer Maria Rilke, Georges Simenon, Ingrid Bergman, Coco Chanel: famous politicians and artists from around the world came there to relax and receive tailor-made treatments. In the 1980s, the Clinique Valmont was the first clinic in Switzerland entirely dedicated to plastic surgery.

In 1985, building on their medical expertise and proven attentiveness to clients' needs, cosmetologists created the first Valmont cellular skincare range by selecting the most active molecules to regenerate the skin. A few years later, the current president, Didier Guillon, began the acquisition of Valmont cosmetics on behalf of a group (which owned the brand Mustela, created by Guillon's father).

He fell in love with both the brand and Switzerland, and from then on worked to develop the brand globally. Since 1996, he has been the sole owner and runs the business with his wife, extolling the virtues of his new homeland, along with a long-term vision, expertise, training, and natural resources. In 2015, Valmont will celebrate its 30th anniversary. Over the years, the brand has become closer and closer to its clientele.

Amongst other things, it has developed an important line of business with spa hotels, offering increasingly professional treatments in line with its image. Today, around 90 products with high-end formulations and over 20 professional treatments are sold at 2,200 points of sale and spas in 43 different markets. The company employs nearly 200 people through a dozen subsidiaries and other channels.

"Whilst in France, make-up, perfume and cosmetic lines have often been created by fashion designers, in Switzerland it is clinical expertise that forms the DNA of cellular cosmetics." Didier Guillon.

OBSERVING WOMAN TO MAKE THEM RADIANT

Sophie Van-Guillon, who runs the company with her husband, is an invaluable link between the laboratories and the brand's clientele. Partly as she manages the research projects as well as designing and promoting new products. And partly because her innate powers of observation help her identify changes in women's habits and environments around the world; she doesn't hesitate to draw inspiration from what she sees. Her enthusiasm for ever more innovative products makes Valmont a pioneer. In 2003, the Radiance range was already offering the kind of glow that has now become the norm. Always ahead of the game, in 2015 she will be working to adapt to different skin types on a global scale.

"Whatever time and resources we invest, our only objective is the – if possible, quick – result: healthy, glowing skin. A radiant woman is a beautiful woman." Sophie Vann-Guillon.

NATURE AND EXPERTISE FOR VISIBLE RESULTS

For around thirty years, Valmont has been innovating to preserve women's health and beauty.
The 'Magicien du Temps' is continuing the Swiss medical tradition and strengthening its heritage by drawing on precious natural resources from its home country and the latest advances in cellular cosmetics to develop effective anti-ageing skincare.

Glacial Spring Water / Thanks to its ideal levels of minerals, glacial spring water encourages tissue exchange, revitalises cells' metabolism and stimulates the skin's natural defences. Gathered at an altitude of more than 6500 feet, at an exclusive site at the foot of the Valais glaciers, it is included in the composition of skin care products just as nature intended: pure, gentle and perfectly balanced.

Essential Plant Extracts / In Vens, deep in the Swiss Alps, Valmont has created a unique space: the phyto-alpine garden. It is in this pure, exclusive environment that the company cultivates the plants chosen for their beneficial effects on the skin. This allows Valmont to control the quality of the extracts destined for its products.

Beneficial active ingredients / Targeting the zones that show the first signs of ageing (face, eyes, décolleté, hands and hair), Valmont selects and formulates ingredients with proven benefits. Native collagen from jellyfish, HP (highly polymerized) DNA, RNA, triple-stranded DNA and liposome DNA lend Valmont's cosmetics their hydrating, antioxidant and energising properties, and their exceptional powers of cellular regeneration.

Basic research plays a key role at Valmont, where the creation of a new range can take three to four years. It combines natural resources and cutting-edge extraction techniques with the help of the best specialists such as dermatologists, biologists and biochemists.

"Artistic work is at the heart of the brand's iconography, which we developed in-house. Art is also a marketing tool that is stronger and more subtle than promotional posters. Works and temporary exhibitions create a special atmosphere for our spa clients. This means we can grab people's attention intelligently and build the brand's profile in a different way."
Didier Guillon, Valmont CEO.

THE SPAS: HARMONIOUS REFUGES IN THE MOST BEAUTIFUL HOTELS IN THE WORLD

The Valmont spas remain faithful to the brand's underlying values, perpetuating the tradition for attentiveness and a close relationship with a demanding clientele. Designed in a contemporary chalet style with warm, natural materials, these havens of peace are nestled in the world's most prestigious hotels. They propose exclusive, professional treatments and a moment of harmony between body and mind. The brand has dozens of establishments, from Verbier to Hong Kong, New York, Russia and Japan.

ART, BEAUTY AND HARMONY

Didier Guillon became interested in contemporary art from a young age and made his passion into a marketing tool for the opening of his business. He integrated this dimension into its graphic identity: a strongly dynamic elegance composed of light and texture. He curates a selection of works for the Valmont spas in the four corners of the world and now combines exhibition-events with worthy projects, such as protecting nature or charitable works.

VALMONT BEAUTY RITUALS

Beauty regimes for morning and evening have been developed to treat the main signs of skin ageing:
Hydration Ritual to provide the skin with intense, long-lasting hydration
Energy Ritual to boost cellular rejuvenation and restore skin's youthfulness
Radiance & Glow Ritual for a glowing, radiant complexion
Elastin & Prime AWF Ritual to combat wrinkles and loss of firmness

Complementary rituals meet individual needs (mattifying, sensitive skin, UV protection, intensive treatments, specific zones, body, hair, etc.) to effectively control all visible signs of ageing.

z|∎

ZAI

Skiing in its purest form

The company founded in 2003 by ski designer Simon Jacomet in Graubünden, Switzerland, has all the makings of greatness. Zai's raison d'être is a labour of love: to manufacture skis with an uncompromising level of quality, materials and performance. Supported by a small group of enthusiastic investors, Simon Jacomet set up a manufacturing workshop in his home town of Disentis in the heart of the Swiss Alps. A long period of research and development followed, with more than two hundred prototypes built and tested. The first model was launched in 2004. The little factory has been changing the face of modern ski design since, introducing innovative materials, radically progressive assembly techniques and revolutionary technologies. Simon Jacomet's vision was built on pluck and passion, with the objective of redefining conventional ski standards and transcending industrial production in terms of quality, materials and finishes.

THE CORE VALUE: PURE SKI

"*Our credo is to seek the essential to achieve a natural balance. Zai skis include everything that good skis require, and nothing else.*"
Simon Jacomet, founder (right picture).

Born in the Swiss Alps in 1963, Simon Jacomet took to the slopes at the age of three. He later worked as a ski instructor to finance his studies at a Florence-based art school. In the 1990s, following a period as Technical Coach for the Swiss Ski Team, he developed products for international brands such as Salomon and Völkl. Both an athlete and an artist, Jacomet brings a fresh approach to ski design. His aesthetic is markedly influenced by the unity of mind, action and substance present in Zen philosophy. "Zai" is Rhaetian - a language spoken in the remote Alpine regions of Switzerland - for "solid". The term also implies "resilience" and "conviction". Zai has carved its own path to the cutting edge of design, development and manufacture. Its pursuit of the essential reveals fluidity and a natural balance between body and equipment. Forget attention-grabbing logos and showy graphics: for Zai, form is based on function, and good design speaks for itself. The pure essence of Zai skis - and the delight of the people who use them - arises from these durable, intrinsic characteristics. All over the world, these exceptional skis are prized by skiers of every level, from beginners to Olympic champions.

"I used to ski. Now that I have discovered Zai, I fly."
Antonio Banderas, actor.

MANUFACTURE: WHEN CRAFTSMANSHIP AND NATURE MEET STATE-OF-THE-ART TECHNOLOGY.

Zai skis are manufactured in the Disentis workshop in the heart of the Swiss Alps, taking inspiration from the rugged landscapes of the Surselva Valley. Unlike other brands, Zai does not develop skis using virtual techniques. Instead, real prototypes are made and tested in various snow conditions by skiers of all ages and levels. The surrounding mountains are the testing grounds for Zai skis at every stage of their development. This process is costly and time-consuming compared to computer-assisted design, but the result is a ski better adapted to the body's movement, the environment, and the perpetual communion between the two.

The factory is both a design workshop and a cutting-edge laboratory. Traditional workmanship is an essential part of the Zai way, imparting quality, authenticity and uniqueness. Zai skis are hand-crafted by local craftsmen for whom wood- and metalwork is a tradition and skiing a way of life. This traditional workmanship is complemented by the factory's high-tech equipment, including one of the most advanced digitally controlled ski presses in the world. Through this approach, blending craftsmanship with state-of-the-art technology, Zai has developed its own unique, innovative assembly methods. Its single objective is to make every pair of skis a masterpiece, no matter how much time, effort and cost the process involves.

Skis such as Testa, with a polished walnut surface; Spada, with a revolutionary stone core; and the limited edition tailor-made Zai for Bentley (designed in collaboration with the legendary car manufacturer) have gained Zai the respect of the most demanding skiers in the world.

In the last few years, Zai has extended its range of products. It now manufactures sunglasses, ski clothing (in cooperation with the Italian fashion house Loro Piana) and golf equipment. All its products are manufactured with the same values of quality, passion and precision. The innovative Zai Senda putter is the latest model from the company's golf line.

With the new edition of Nezza, a ski with a split tail design made with a composite material developed by Zai hand-laid around a cedar-wood core, the brand is reaffirming its pioneer spirit. Offering unique style and incomparable performance, Nezza has quickly gained approval from the most discriminating connoisseurs in the world.

MATERIALS

Zai skis are made using the most refined materials, and they are built to last. Zai is a pioneer in assembly methods and technologies, going so far as to develop tools to meet its own requirements, revolutionising modern ski design. Its avant-garde approach to design can seem miraculous, such as bending stone to produce the famous CFS® stone core, or creating entirely new high-tech materials.

World leader in the use of radically new materials, Zai utilises a widely varied range including such unusual materials as granite, cedar wood, Dyneema® and its own patented carbon fibre, Zaiíra®. For Zai, natural materials such as wood, rubber, leather and stone are perfect counterparts to carbon fibre and cutting-edge metals.

In Zai's function-based logic, each material is used for its specific qualities: cedar wood because it is lightweight and has a high tensile strength; granite because of its compressive strength and excellent shock absorption (for a weight equivalent to that of aluminium); natural rubber because it is scratch- and weather-proof, and provides shock absorption; quenched steel because it resists corrosion. All these materials can be reworked to a like-new finish when the ski is serviced at the end of each season. The stainless steel upper edges add durability and can be reworked in the grinding process – a feature unique to Zai skis. By combining these materials in revolutionary ways, Zai attains handling ability, durability and performance far beyond the conventional levels. Mass-produced skis lose around 25% of their tension after just thirty days of use, while Zai skis lose just 5% after a hundred days. It is technological leaps such as this which have helped Zai to redefine the standards of ski design.

zimmerli
of Switzerland

ZIMMERLI

A Manufacture for high-quality, sophisticated textiles

Since 1871, Zimmerli of Switzerland has drawn on its sophisticated expertise in order to refine its creations – producing woven and knitted underwear from natural fibres of exceptional quality, in Switzerland. The company is distinguished by its approach to seeking out technical innovations, and for its outstanding quality and careful selection of the highest-grade materials. Zimmerli is known for its inimitable products and attaches great importance to the fact that they are manufactured in Switzerland. The company has grown along with its success and is based on the values consistent with its reputation and the high-quality products for which it is known. Today, Zimmerli enjoys a loyal customer base made up of important and cultured connoisseurs drawn by the timeless elegance of the brand, and continues to strive to uphold its unique promise: "The world's finest underwear. Handmade in Switzerland since 1871."

REPUTATION AND EXPANSION: A LONG-TERM STRATEGY

Zimmerli continues to build its notoriety using a long-term strategy. This approach is systematically implemented at all levels. The focus is on the core of the brand, which informs not only the contemporary brand image, but also the way the company is organised and its sales policy. The focal points of the strategic brand development

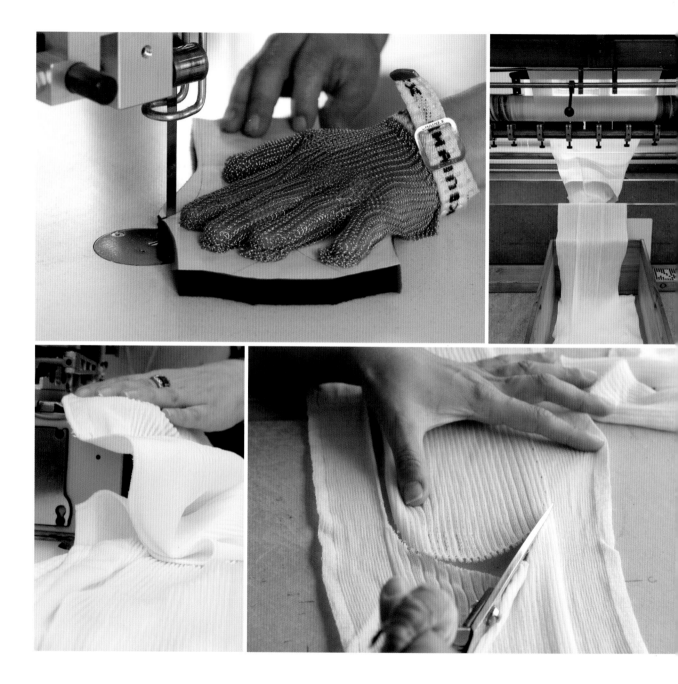

are concentrated on Europe, the United States, Russia and China – those markets in which it already enjoys representation through collaboration with excellent partners. The clients include major department stores, underwear and fashion boutiques and, more recently, a number of own-brand boutiques. Zimmerli is represented only in the world's choicest places, thus emphasising the exclusive nature of the brand and strengthening the pursuit of its goals. This group of partners includes highclass addresses such as KadeWe, Harrods, Jelmoli and Barneys in New York. It now boasts around 650 corporate clients in 40 countries.

ESSENTIAL VALUES FOR LONG-TERM SUCCESS

Extraordinary and noticeable quality / The brand stands for a high-value and distinctive quality that is visible and perceptible even to non-experts.

Fine materials / The manufacture of the finest underwear only uses materials made from precious natural fibres.

Timeless underwear for everyday use / Zimmerli products are not fashionable but a guarantee of elegance, with their classic, clean cut and lines.

Hand-made products / The tailors work with the utmost care and precision – an anachronism which also represents an incomparable privilege.

Switzerland / The head office of the traditional Zimmerli Manufacture is still located in Switzerland, where it has been since 1871.

THE CHALLENGES OF PRODUCTION IN SWITZERLAND

Zimmerli strives on a daily basis to attain the best possible quality of materials and products that can be seen and felt, and to do this with the help of a contented and committed workforce, who love their job. Every week, 55 tailors in the Canton of Ticino carefully prepare several thousand articles. Up to 18 manufacturing steps are required until the underwear is completed in Switzerland and sent for export around the world. As Zimmerli produces its underwear exclusively in Switzerland, it incurs significantly higher labour costs than elsewhere. This disadvantage is offset by a first-class business service, high flexibility and impeccable quality. The company's clear commitment to Switzerland as the site of its operations lies behind the company's steady growth over the years.

THE ZIMMERLI SUCCESS STORY

The Zimmerli story began in 1871 with the purchase of a hand-operated knitting machine by Pauline Zimmerli, a native of Aarburg, who used the machine to produce high-quality stockings. Her foresight and long-term vision enabled her to acquire further machines and her goods were sold as far away as Paris. She was soon producing fine rib woven fabric and underwear and laid the foundation for a whole new industry. Elastic-grade "Swiss fine rib textiles" were invented by Pauline Zimmerli and brought her great success and worldwide fame. The fine rib articles earned a Gold Medal at the Universal Exhibition in 1889, and in 1900 Zimmerli picked up the Grand Prix itself. In 1965, the company took over a production workshop in Coldrerio in the Canton of Ticino. It is there that the Zimmerli tailors – amongst the most qualified and talented anywhere – produce the "world's most refined lingerie."

THREE NEW COLLECTIONS

AVA / with Calais lace

This particularly feminine line boasts an embroidered floral design and a weft of Calais tulle. The mercerised, meshed cotton lends itself superbly to the contours of the body.

MADISON / the simple language of shapes

This range, distinguished by its classical and sporty elegance, is made without side seams and hugs the figure perfectly thanks to its 6x6 rib. The mercerised and breathable cotton can also be worn as an outdoor shirt.

PIQUÉ COMO / this symbiosis of two materials

This double fabric combines cotton and MicroModal. The combination of these two materials gives the underwear a natural grip and provides optimal moisture transfer. Spandex also maintains the correct shape. "Pikee" is a material with a subtle surface relief that enjoys a high degree of robustness. The hidden seams underline the high quality work of the Manufacture.

✚ SWISS

SWISS

Flying the flag for the Swiss economy

Swiss International Air Lines (SWISS) is Switzerland's national airline, serving 84 destinations in 40 countries from Zurich, Basel and Geneva and carrying over 16 million passengers a year with its 90-aircraft fleet. The company's Swiss WorldCargo airfreight business unit, meanwhile, provides a comprehensive range of airport-to-airport cargo services for high-value and intensive-care consignments to about 120 destinations in over 80 countries, along with supplementary road feeder services.

As the airline of Switzerland, SWISS embodies the country's traditional values, and is committed to delivering the highest product and service quality. With its manageable medium size, SWISS is also optimally equipped to remain as close as possible to its customers and meet their individual needs. With its workforce of some 8,250 personnel, SWISS generated total operating income for 2013 of CHF 5.17 billion. SWISS is committed on various fronts to the careful and sustainable use of natural resources, and regards a responsible attitude to the environment as an integral part of its corporate culture. As part of the Lufthansa Group and a member of Star Alliance, SWISS remains faithful to its mission of providing quality air services that link Switzerland with Europe and the world.

AWARDS

Swiss International Air Lines has been named "Europe's Leading Airline Business Class" in the 2014 World Travel Awards for the fourth time in a row. It has also taken first place in the "Best Business Class Catering" category in the Skytrax World Airline Awards 2012. The annual industry distinctions are based on a survey of several million air travellers by the UK-based Skytrax consultancy company. In 2011 SWISS earned the Skytrax World Airline Award as "Best Airline for Western Europe". SWISS won further top honours in 2011, too. These "Best First Class Seat" in the Global Traveler Awards, the second year in succession that it has earned such a distinction for its First Class product. This award by the US-based Global Traveler magazine, followed a poll of more than 25,000 frequent and premium flyers worldwide.

SWISS INVESTING IN FURTHER FLEET RENEWAL

CSeries: a quantum leap in noise reduction

Toward the end of 2015 SWISS will begin introducing the brand new Bombardier CSeries aircraft as the successor to its existing Avro RJ100 fleet, which numbers 20 aircraft. The new aircraft type applies the latest advances in engine, systems and materials technology to set new standards in terms of profitability and environmental compatibility. Fuel consumption compared to the Avro fleet will be reduced by as much as one quarter. Further, in terms of human auditory sensitivity the new aircraft generates only half the noise level of its predecessor.

Thanks to innovation in cabin design, passengers can look forward to a significant increase in travel comfort.

Airbus A340 fleet to be replaced with six Boeing 777-300ERs

SWISS will begin replacing its present long-haul aircraft fleet from 2016 onwards. To this end, orders have been placed for six Boeing 777-300ER aircraft. The decision to opt for Boeing's successful 777 was taken after extensive evaluations. The six firm orders represent a total investment of more than CHF 1.5 billion.

The new Boeing twinjets will be deployed on SWISS's ultra-long-range routes to destinations such as San Francisco, Los Angeles, São Paulo, Bangkok, Hong Kong, Shanghai, Beijing, Johannesburg and Singapore.

SWISS provides optimal connections from Switzerland to the main European and intercontinental centres. With economic growth increasingly taking place beyond Europe, SWISS is of ever greater importance to Switzerland's economy.

SWISSNESS

As the airline of Switzerland, SWISS puts a clear and keen emphasis on the quality of the food and beverages that it serves aboard its flights. To this end, SWISS works closely and continuously with Swiss-based producers and top chefs from all over the country to present a range of inflight food that showcases the best of Switzerland's cuisine. With its award-winning "SWISS Taste of Switzerland" inflight culinary programme and its "SWISS Traditions" concept for its European services, SWISS offers regional specialities from all over the country aboard its flights. At the same time, SWISS also collaborates with renowned hotels around the world to offer dishes of equally outstanding quality to its guests from other cultures. The result of all these endeavours is a range of inflight fare that deftly reflects both SWISS's strong Swiss roots and the global scope of its air travel services. The innovative "SWISS Taste of Switzerland" inflight foodservice concept was launched back in December 2002. The programme puts a culinary spotlight on a different part of Switzerland every three months, offering a totally new selection of dishes each time that are devised by a renowned Swiss chef from the guest canton and boast a distinctly regional touch. In February 2012 SWISS further expanded its range of inflight fare with the new "SWISS Traditions" programme, under which Business Class travellers on European flights are served classic and popular Swiss delights together with dishes that have their roots in famous national and cultural events. SWISS thus offers its guests not just fine Swiss food but a taste of the country's heritage, too. Four times each year the "SWISS Traditions" programme provides a two-week celebration of a particular Swiss institution.

Volume by the numbers: SWISS distributes some 16.2 million chocolate bars to passengers annually.

FREITAG

From truck till bag

In 1993, two graphic designers, Markus and Daniel Freitag, were looking for a bag which was functional, water-repellent and heavy-duty for carrying their sketches. Inspired by the multicoloured heavy goods traffic in Zurich, they developed a shoulder bag made from old truck tarpaulins, bike inner tubes and used seat belts. This is how the first FREITAG bags were born, in the living room of the two brothers' flatshare. Over 20 years later, FREITAG bags are cut out from lorry tarpaulins which have done their time. The challenge? Finding enough old tarpaulins to make 400,000 products a year! This is why logistics are essential: they're directed by a team of five people who buy 440 tonnes of used tarpaulins every year (or 110km of lorries) from Sweden to Portugal, as well as 35,000 bike inner tubes and 288,000 seat belts.

PRODUCTION STEPS AND SURPRISING CAREERS

In order to transform the grubby road scrap into a raw material destined to be a prized bag needs, the gigantic lengths of tarpaulin must first be disassembled. Armed with knives and grinders, the dismantlers take the straps, buckles and metal parts off the dirty tarpaulins. A difficult job and a career that only exists at FREITAG! Then the selected pieces are washed to get rid of the road dirt and reveal their unique shine. For this, some

AN AVALANCHE OF PRIZES

The company has gained impressive status in every respect since it was founded. Whether for its designs or its marketing, the architecture of its stores or its web presence, FREITAG has cleaned up with prizes by the dozen. Here are some examples:

2014 European Design Awards, gold for the REFERENCE product catalogues "AGED 10 YEARS".

2013 "SwissAward" 2012 in the Business category.

2012 GfM marketing prize : Annual prize from the Foundation for Marketing in Corporate Management.

2011 Design Prize Switzerland MERIT for continuous services in the field of design for Daniel and Markus Freitag.

2008 Gold for the FREITAG Flagship Store in Zurich at the 8th International contractworld award. 1st prize for Marketing and Architecture for the FREITAG Flagship Store in Zurich. Best of Swiss Web: Gold seal in the Business Efficiency category, Silver seal in the Creation category, Bronze seal in the Technology Quality category.

2007 D&AD Global Awards, Golden Pencil for Environmental Design/Retail & Services.

2005 F12 DRAGNET bag was presented at the Who's Next Fashion trade show in Paris as one of the milestones of "urban fashion".

2003 The original F13 TOP CAT model was accepted into the design collection of the Museum of Modern Art in New York (MoMA).

1999 Distinction awarded in the Trade Competition for Applied Arts.

1997 1993 prototype was accepted in the collection of the Zurich Museum of Design. Distinction, Design Prize Switzerland.

4 million litres of water per year are needed. Therefore, rainwater is collected from the F-actory roof so that no fresh water is wasted. The heat from the dirty water is transferred to the cooler and cleaner rainwater, so that much of the energy needed for heating can be saved. Though new models are created in the official design department, the cutting is also the work of a bag designer, done entirely by hand. Using a Stanley knife and a stencil, the designers choose the best parts of the tarpaulins and cut out each part of the bag. A strange job for a unique product.

UNIQUE URBAN PRODUCTS

Each FREITAG bag, whether cut from tarpaulins or other recycled materials, is unique due to the individual cutting of the tarpaulin and the patina from the street.
Inspired by the first messenger bag F13 TOP CAT, the functional FUNDAMENTALS product line today offers over 40 different models, from smartphone cases to shopping bags, from notebook sleeves to rucksacks.

Using a Stanley knife and a stencil, the designers choose the best parts of the tarpaulins and cut out each part of the bag.

The FREITAG REFERENCE collection, created in 2010, offers around fifteen top-end models crafted from vintage lorry tarpaulins.

AN IDEA THAT'S TRAVELLED THE WORLD

Without really meaning to, the two brothers started a global trend and have become immensely successful. Expanding out of Switzerland, people know their bags in Asia and other European capital cities, making FREITAG the unofficial outfitter of all cycling urban individualists.

As creative directors and owners of their company, Daniel and Markus Freitag still design, develop, and follow up on every new model until its final stage of production to this day. They have a team of around 160 employees. FREITAG products are distributed throughout the world, supported by 470 sales partners, around ten FREITAG boutiques in Switzerland, Germany, Austria and Japan, and an online shop.

Since 2011, the general headquarters of lorry tarpaulin bags has been in the Maison des métiers Noerd in Zurich-Oerlikon.

LAURASTAR

Full steam ahead

Laurastar's story begins in 1980 when its founder, who had a passion for beautiful fabrics, decided to collaborate with an Italian engineer. One of them was an aesthete, the other had a dream: to make technology - previously limited to professionals - accessible to all. Their passion gave rise to a new era where Swiss technology could be used to care for and enhance clothing at home. Their first creation was an ironing board with an integrated professional generator. An easy-to-use steam-press that gave impeccable results had made its way into the home. Laurastar made professional ironing systems available to everyone and they proved popular with the general public from the word go. Laurastar's researchers, engineers and designers have been making efficiency and simplicity synonymous for over 30 years. Attaching the utmost importance to their products' shape, colour and ergonomic design, they work constantly to remain at the cutting edge. Their increasingly innovative products reflect the company's strong values: quality, precision and aestheticism. These values contribute to the reputation for excellence that the Swiss enjoy the world over. Today, Laurastar is the world leader in professional ironing systems for the home. The company based in Châtel-Saint-Denis in the canton of Fribourg exports 70% of its production, 53% of which is exported to Europe. Over 2 million products are sold in more than forty countries.

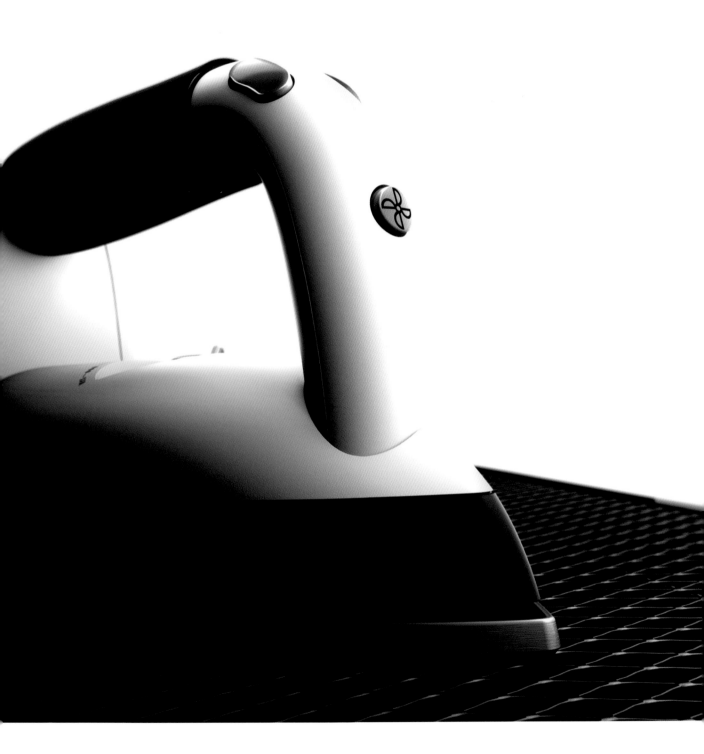

LAURASTAR'S TECHNOLOGIES

The 3D active soleplate

It provides unparalleled quality in a single sweep of the iron thanks to its double action: the raised section on the iron's soleplate holds the fabric taut while the steam injected over the surface effortlessly eliminates creases.

An exclusive steam system

Laurastar specialises in ultra-fine yet powerful steam and equips these cutting-edge, top-of-the-range models with pulsed steam, for the very best care for your clothes. The steam is diffused by successive automatic pulses, guaranteeing the ideal dosage for a perfect result, whatever the colour or fabric.

Active ironing board

The ironing boards are equipped with a 2-speed blower and vacuum system to prevent creasing and protect fabric. You can change from the 'blower to 'vacuum' mode at the touch of a button.

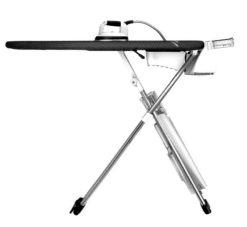

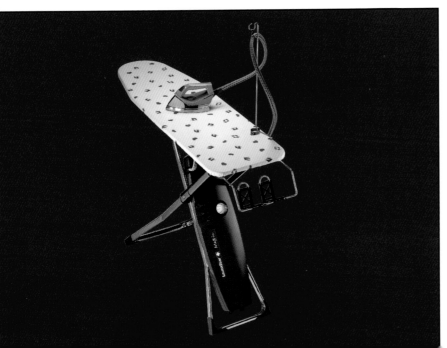

1 000 000 - OVER A MILLION
IRONING SYSTEMS SOLD

Laurastar Magic, a Swiss innovation, is the first ironing
system for home use to include an ironing board that
both sucks in and blows out air to prevent creasing
and protect fabric. Since it was created in 1996, this
Swiss technology has brought about a small revolution. It is the brand's flagship product and more than a
million have been sold. Today this system has evolved
further with the creation of the Laurastar Go range.

SWISS EXPERTISE,
THE HEIGHT OF EXCELLENCE

The company has revolutionised ironing techniques by ingeniously combining the power of iron, steam and air. Its expertise lies in harnessing this power to make caring for clothes increasingly simple and ergonomic. This is why Swiss researchers and engineers are constantly innovating to turn state-of-the-art technology into an everyday tool. With professional irons, 3D active soleplates, exclusive ultra-fine steam, active boards - Laurastar's ironing systems have one aim: to make it easy for anyone to care for and enhance their fabrics. In order to uphold and guarantee the brand's values, each product is tested in a lab for almost 1000 hours until unbeatable usability and an exceptional result can be ensured.

LAURASTAR LIFT: THE FIRST
EVER PORTABLE GENERATOR

The Laurastar Lift steam generator is the result of five years of research and development, and combines technology with ultra-functional design. It revolutionises traditional ironing methods.

Laurastar Lift is compact, lightweight and has a handle, making it very easy to manipulate. The generator is easily transported from one room to another, meaning you take it to the clothes and not the other way round, combining performance with intuitive design. This means you can remove the creases from a curtain or a jacket on a hanger quickly and effortlessly, as well as ironing a shirt on the board. Laurastar Lift is ready to use in just three minutes, and stops automatically after 10 minutes of inaction.

This next-generation steam generator is also a contemporary, sophisticated piece of design, devised by Antoine Cahen, an industrial designer from the Ateliers du Nord in Lausanne. It is available in a range of eight colours.

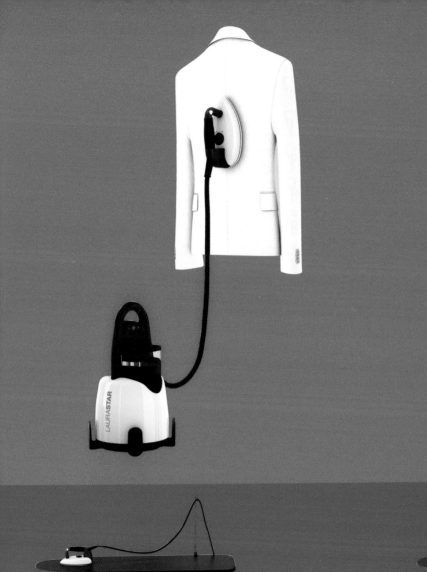

DESIGN AND INNOVATION

Innovation and top ergonomics are the company's main concerns when designing its products. This policy has earned the brand regular recognition, for both its design and its technological advances.

1999 Good Design Award, from the Chicago Athenaeum Museum of Architecture and Design

2001 Silver medal, Concours Lépine in Paris

2002 Red Dot Design Award, Best of the Best category

2012 Technology Award 2012 Foire de Paris Innovation Awards

2013 Red Dot Design Award, Product Design category

2013 Good Design Australia

2014 Good Design Award, from the Chicago Athenaeum Museum of Architecture and Design

LOGITECH

A technological pioneer

For over 30 years, Logitech products have won consumers over with their mix of artistic design, science and visionary innovation. Logitech connects people to their favourite digital experiences, and is one of the main international suppliers of computer and tablet accessories (peripheral devices for computers, keyboards, mice, etc.) Logitech's hardware and software solutions are available for numerous computer, communications and gaming platforms and enhance digital navigation, audio and video entertainment, gaming, social networking, communication over the internet and controlling multimedia equipment in the home.

As well as its head offices in Switzerland and the USA, Logitech also has offices in Europe, Asia and in the rest of the Americas. Its sales and marketing activities are organised into three geographical regions: the Americas, EMEA and Asia-Pacific.

Logitech International is a Swiss public company, listed on the SIX Swiss Exchange (LOGN) and on the Nasdaq Global Select Market (LOGI). Its turnover is close to 2 billion Swiss francs.

NEW MOUSE

Logitech recently unveiled the G402 Hyperion Fury, the fastest gaming mouse ever created. It is equipped with extremely precise, programmable sensors and is thrilling gamers.

HISTORY

Logitech International S.A. was co-founded in 1981 by two Stanford graduates, Daniel Borel and Pierluigi Zappacosta. At first, the company set itself up in Apples, in the Swiss canton of Vaud, in an old farm belonging to Daniel Borel's in-laws, where it designed graphics software. Part of the development side of the business was soon transferred to Silicon Valley. During these early years, Logitech occupied offices at 165 University Avenue in Palo Alto, California, an address known for having been home to a number of tech start-ups. Logitech developed its range of products to include a number of peripheral devices. Its main asset: the mouse. At the time, it was a new development that finally provided a more intuitive way to interact with computers. In Switzerland, Daniel Borel starting making a mouse based on the first prototypes. (Originally invented by Douglas Engelbart, the idea had already been reworked by engineers from the EPFL Institute of Technology in Lausanne). The first generation was made by the company Dubois Dépraz SA in the Vallée de Joux, Switzerland, a company that was also a well-known supplier of chronographs for Swiss watchmakers.

From 1984 onwards, Logitech's client base included Hewlett-Packard and the company experienced a meteoric rise, becoming the world leader in computer mice, which were selling in large numbers.

In 1996, it recorded one million mouse sales. Twelve years later, the company passed the billion mark. These figures are a perfect illustration of the explosion of the global computer market.

DIVERSIFYING TO STAY ON TOP

Logitech has been at the origin of a large number of innovations. Thanks to products sold in nearly every country around the world, Logitech's dominant position currently includes a large range of personal peripherals (wireless and corded). Designers and engineers work to improve these peripherals to make them ever more functional, user-friendly, fun, productive and attractive.

Logitech Harmony – programmable remote controls.

Logitech G – gaming line.

Logitech cases and accessories for tablets and smartphones.

The Ultimate Ears range groups together all the products relating to digital music

Logitech computer peripherals including mice, keyboards, webcams, speakers for PCs, keyboards for tablets, etc.

ULTIMATE EARS

Logitech brand Ultimate Ears has been revolutionising musician's onstage performances since 1995 by developing professional, tailor-made earplugs. The products have now become a favourite amongst performers: earphones and speakers lauded by critics for the excellent acoustic experience they offer. Ultimate Ears is the leading manufacturer of in-ear monitors customised for professional musicians, and is also making its mark as a high-end speaker and headphone supplier on the mass market.

INNOVATION AND PRICE

Logitech's products – in all its ranges – have been showered with accolades for their innovation and design, almost on a yearly basis. The company regularly wins the Red Dot Award or the iF Product Design Award, the CES Innovation Award or the Good Design Award... to name but a few.

A music speaker, the UE Boom from Ultimate Ears, has also been specially designed for listening socially, with a 360° sound diffusion, an above average battery life and suitability for network use.

ON

Shoes that enhance your performance

Since his retirement from active sport, two-time biathlon world champion and multiple Ironman winner Olivier Bernhard has dedicated himself to a new passion: the development of running shoes that provide an optimum running sensation. His path soon crossed that of a Swiss engineer, thus creating the perfect combination of engineering science and running experience. The development phase was very long and the cupboards were stuffed with prototypes – all based on the same concept: a soft landing and a firm push-off. And although the first version was assembled using pieces of garden hose, the company now offers models that enjoy an international reputation.

This basic concept and the search for that unique running sensation convinced Caspar Coppetti and David Allemann to team up with Bernhard. After they tried On for themselves, they were equally convinced about the innovation. In January 2010, they co-founded their company in Zurich, in order to design a product line that was completely made in Switzerland based on the latest technologies. Events followed very quickly after that. The prototypes won the ISPO Brand New Award in February – one of the most important innovation prizes in sport. Test runners were enthusiastic and compared the result to running on clouds. In July 2010, the first speciality shops were stocking the shoes on their shelves. Today, five years later, On is sold in over 1300 running speciality

stores in more than 25 countries, and the brand has won design and technology prizes around the world.

OPTIMISING THE PERFORMANCE OF ATHLETES

Having made waves throughout the running scene, the shoes are now enjoying increasing popularity with professional sports men and women, bringing them new personal bests at World Championships. The quality of On shoes is appreciated by athletes all over the world, from Switzerland to England and France, and from Africa to the USA (Nicola Spirig, Caroline Steffen, Ben Allen, David Hauss, Tegla Loroupe, Frederik Van Lierde, Lesley Paterson, Jacqui Slack, Mary Beth Ellis...)
The shoes are also used by the Swiss SAUBER Formula One team.

BREAKTHROUGH TECHNOLOGY

After over a century of different concepts in the sport of running, On has developed and patented the CloudTec® system, which absorbs impact and helps runners roll naturally onto the forefoot. The Cloud components remain firm, providing stability and giving a powerful kick. The numerous cloud components, distributed all over the sole, adjust to the runner's movements and respond accordingly. These reactions take place either in unison or separately, in order to absorb the shock. On shoes also ensure that the

A RESOUNDING SUCCESS IN JUST A FEW YEARS

2005-2009 Along with a Swiss engineer, Olivier Bernhard developed a running shoe with superb cushioning using «Cloud» technology.

2010 The introduction of the Cloudrunner with optimised cushioning. A study published by the Swiss Federal Institute of Technology in Zurich (Eidgenössische Technische Hochschule Zürich) showed that test runners using On shoes ran with a significantly lower pulse rate and blood lactate levels. Shortly after its introduction, the On was available in 400 specialist shops in 18 countries, including the USA, Australia, South Korea and Singapore.

2012 The launch of the Cloudster, followed by the Cloudracer — a running shoe developed especially for competition. The French athlete David Hauss posted the third best running time in the triathlon at the London Olympics in On shoes. The Wall Street Journal described On as a revolutionary running shoe.

2013 The CloudTec® system is constantly improving with new Swiss technology. With its new Cloudrunner model, On launched a new flexplate named Speedboard. On picked up the 2013 ISPO Gold Award for best shoe performances well as the coveted Swiss Design Prize for avant-garde designs. Kenya's Geoffrey Gikuni Ndungu won the Jungfrau Marathon in On Cloudracers. The event is Europe's most popular mountain marathon. The Belgian Frederik Van Lierde won the 2014 Ironman World championship in Kona, Hawaii wearing the new Cloudracer. In addition to its head office in Zurich, On opened a second base in Portland, Oregon.

2014 With the On Cloud, the brand launches the world's lightest fully cushioned running shoe.

central point of impact is in the middle of the foot, the natural equilibrium point of the body. In other words, On absorbs the shock only when needed, thus delaying fatigue and supporting the natural running style. A philosophy that is confirmed by the latest findings in biomechanical research. .

On offers a selection of shoes adapted to different needs, from the On Cloudster to the On Cloudracer.

Cloudster / A running shoe for everyday use, equipped with the original CloudTec® system, ensuring a soft landing.

Cloudrunner / A running shoe for demanding on and off-road racing. The CloudTec® rubber system ensures a longer life for the sole without abrasion. The upper reinforcement provides extra protection and a comfortable fit.

Cloudsurfer / The running shoe for increasing performance. Light and smooth, it transforms running energy into a forward thrust, both during training and in competition.

Cloudracer / With its 18 low-profile rubber components, the CloudTec® system of the Cloudracer is designed for competition and is distinguished by its ultra-light structure. The specially designed mesh-webbing and the ultra-fine tongue hold the foot with minimum weight.

Cloud / A minimalistic and light shoe with maximum flexibility and cushioning.

Top left: Cloud
Top right: Cloudster
Bottom left: Cloudracer
Bottom right: Cloudsurfer

SIGG™ ⊕

SIGG

The drinking bottle that refreshes the world

The SIGG company, founded in Switzerland over 100 years ago, has evolved from a manufacturer of household aluminium articles into a truly iconic brand. Its aluminium bottles have become genuine must-have items. Throughout the world, modern globetrotters quench their thirst using original SIGG bottles, which are found everywhere from children's backpacks to the bags of hipsters at yoga class, at lovers' picnics or executive business lunches. Thanks to its practical design and lightness, the bottle forms part of the basic equipment of thrill-seeking mountain climbers. And above and beyond such lofty heights, it has become an indispensable accessory for film stars and top models alike.

THE PERFECT COMPANION ON ANY TERRAIN

SIGG bottles are innovative, functional, perfect when on the move and ideal for sport and leisure pursuits. The body of the traditional SIGG bottle is seamlessly extruded from a single piece of pure aluminium. The bright colours are produced by solvent-free powder coating. The inner coating is not only elastic and tear-resistant but also guaranteed taste-neutral and resistant to fruit acids or isotonic drinks. It takes 26 forming steps to transform an aluminium cylinder into a SIGG bottle with a threaded ring. In

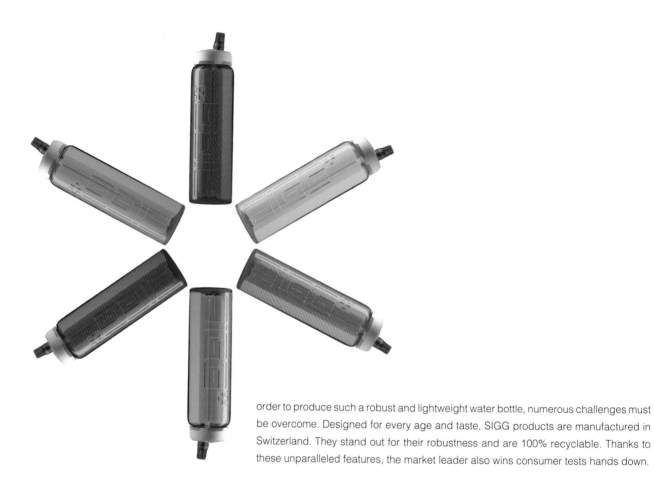

order to produce such a robust and lightweight water bottle, numerous challenges must be overcome. Designed for every age and taste, SIGG products are manufactured in Switzerland. They stand out for their robustness and are 100% recyclable. Thanks to these unparalleled features, the market leader also wins consumer tests hands down.

ART AND DESIGN OBJECT

This iconic object is much more than just a simple bottle. It serves as a canvas for artists, as proved by a number of masterpieces that have won places in the world's greatest museums. In 1993, the inclusion of SIGG in the collection of the Museum of Modern Arts (MOMA) in New York proved that the design of everyday objects is a true art. In making its products, SIGG regularly collaborates with the most prestigious design agencies, who have won renown for their expertise, new technologies and creative concepts. In 2014 SIGG picked up a Red Dot Award for its SIGG HOT & COLD collection. This label, which enjoys a very high reputation worldwide, serves to distinguish the most innovative quality products. This product design competition is one of the most demanding in the world. An international jury of 40 design experts spent several days assessing the submitted products – this year saw no fewer than 4,815 submissions.

SIGG VIVA

Transparent and eco conscious.

The water bottles of the new SIGG VIVA collection are made of high-quality and recyclable polypropylene. Like their sister aluminium products, VIVA bottles are produced according to the same quality and environmental criteria in Switzerland. However, they have one very significant difference: they are transparent!

HISTORY

1908 Establishment of a factory in Biel by Ferdinand Sigg, which produces household items made of aluminium, especially chamber pots and bottles.

1917 The company headquarters moves to Frauenfeld and the name is changed to SIGG AG Aluminiumwarenfabrik. The company expands its product range and conquers the European market. In the post-war period, the shortage of raw material proves to be the mother of invention. SIGG manages to produce water and hot water bottles from waste material. The first drafts of the «Original Bottle», which enjoys iconic status to this day.

1958 The range includes several thousand household articles and items of sports equipment.

1980 The first monochrome painted bottle paves the way for a series of innovative and colourful products.

In recent years, SIGG became a leading provider of hydration solutions with subsidaries in Germany, North America and China, as well as offices in the UK and Austria. SIGG bottles are available in over 40 countries worldwide. The brand's competence is amply demonstrated through its core values. Each year, the extensive collection of functional, durable and contemporary water bottles is adapted and expanded in line with current trends.

Fabulous Ladies

CUIPO

MSF

Swiss Emblem Red

SIGG HOT & COLD

Functional. Minimalist. Contemporary.

SIGG HOT & COLD bottles combine insulating technology with a contemporary look. Made of high-quality 18/8 stainless steel (chosen because of its structural properties and resistance to corrosion) and equipped with vacuum insulation, achieved by a double stainless steel wall with applied copper and zirconium in between, the SIGG isothermal bottle is ideal for the safe storage of hot and cold drinks, as it keeps their temperature for hours.

DISTINCTIONS

In 2014 SIGG picked up a Red Dot Award for its SIGG HOT & COLD collection. This label, which enjoys a very high reputation worldwide, serves to distinguish the most innovative quality products. This product design competition is one of the most demanding in the world. An international jury of 40 design experts spent several days assessing the submitted products – this year saw no fewer than 4,815 submissions.

STÖCKLI

Convincing Swiss Quality

The origin of skiing dates way back in the history of mankind. People used skis to cross the fens in Scandinavia several thousand years ago. This means of transport aroused great enthusiasm amongst the youth of central Europe at the end of the 19th century, when a group of researchers crossed Greenland on "snowshoes". This event marked the beginning of the modern era for skiing. The first ski clubs were founded in Switzerland, and the sport rapidly grew in popularity. At the beginning of the 20th century, skiing became very fashionable, thanks to a group of Norwegians working and studying in Switzerland. The local youth proved very inventive and made their own skis with a few wooden boards. At the beginning of the 1930s, Josef Stöckli tinkered around with a few materials to create his first pair of skis. In order to bend and fashion the wood, which he had sawed in his family carpentry, he fired up his mother's large wash boiler. Even then, the young man stood out for his great spirit of innovation. To make the skis lighter, he removed material from the surface. His "home-made" skis were of high quality and earned him a reputation. In his very first winter, the young ski manufacturer sold around 50 pairs that he had made in his free time. In the face of increasing demand, he founded the «Skifabrik Stöckli AG» in 1935. Of the 30 or so ski factories in Switzerland, «Stöckli Ski» is the only one to have survived to this day.

THE STRADIVARIUS OF SKIS

"Wood is a naturally high-tech material. No synthetic material can match it for elasticity, precision, dynamics or flexibility", says the head of the research and development department at Stöckli, Ruedi Arnet.

Just as a violin maker only uses the best wood to build his instruments, the ski manufacturer chooses the raw materials for his sports equipment with the utmost care. Both in violin-making and ski production, over 100 factors must be harmoniously integrated. The production process is extremely time-consuming in both cases. Despite high-tech developments, wood continues to be of fundamental importance and plays a decisive role in ski production. The qualities of this raw material in terms of its dynamics have often been copied but never matched. Even when combined with other materials, a wood core is still an integral part of almost all Stöckli skis today.

And customers also benefit directly from the innovations created for the high-performance sport models. Skis for Stöckli customers are developed and built by the same people as the skis for top athletes. Today Stöckli skis regularly occupy first place in international ski tests.

A PIONEER OF THE MODERN SKI INDUSTRY

Josef Stöckli, who described himself as a "mad dog" on the piste, was an exceptional craftsman. He only sold what he had previously tested himself, and thus turned his innovative ideas into reality. In 1945 he produced the first skis made of hickory and ash wood. From 1957, along with Head and Attenhofer, he was amongst the pioneers of metal skis. His small factory at the gates of Entlebuch was the only one to market them. It proved a triumph among skiers, and the market boomed. Later, he invented the «knife», in order to prevent the skins on the ski undersurface from slipping sideways during ascent, and the "trapezoidal" ski shape, which was ultimately to prevail in the industry. However, due to the lack of patents, these inventions brought him no wealth.

The company founder followed the development of new models with great interest until shortly before his death in 2010. Turnover, which amounted to about 3 million Swiss francs in 1982, has today achieved a considerable 60 million Swiss francs. The family-run business currently has around 240 permanent employees in its 14 sales outlets. The head office of Stöckli Swiss Sports AG has remained in Wolhusen since the company was founded in 1935.

SKI RACES: THE FROM THE PODIUM TO THE GENERAL PUBLIC

In the 1990s, the company began an entirely new chapter in its history. After long negotiations, Stöckli was appointed the official supplier to the Swiss Ski Pool. Since that time, Swiss athletes have been able to compete at the World Championships on Stöckli skis. The Olympic silver medallist Urs Kälin started the World Championship on these skis as the number one Swiss skier. Swiss champion, as well as achieving victory and runner-up position in the World Championships – in 2013, Stöckli's tireless commitment to better skis reaped the rewards. Stöckli won the World Cup overall title with Tina Maze – thus becoming Switzerland's premier ski producer overall, achieving an unprecedented total of 2,414 World Cup points. The success story continued into 2014. Tina Maze's double Olympic victory in the downhill and giant slalom and the twin victories of Marielle Thompson and Kelsey Serwa in the ski cross testified to the unique expertise of the ski manufacturer from the Swiss canton of Lucerne. Thanks to these decisive results, new perspectives opened up for the manufacturer on the international level. Exports began to boom.

SALES: "QUALITY NOT QUANTITY"

Because he was unable to reach an agreement with sports shops, Josef Stöckli decided to sell his skis directly to customers. He opted for a vertical and direct sales structure, which has remained unchanged since 1967. Thanks to this concept, the margin usually reserved for middlemen directly benefits the customer. And the lack of negotiations with the dealers has also proved to be a great advantage, leaving more time free for the development of new models. A strategy which has brought customers quality performance at affordable prices.

This concept is one of the secrets of the company's success. Even today, Stöckli remains close to its customers in its points of sale. In the wake of the rise in demand following the Ski World Cup in 1995, the brand decided to expand its distribution network. In addition to its 14 stores, 35 hand-picked sports shops were chosen as business partners in Switzerland's major skiing resorts. An exquisite sales strategy that is also applied to the global market. Around 40% of production is currently exported to 32 countries. Austria is one of the biggest markets, even though the country is a world leader in ski production!

OUTDOOR SPORTS

Even though only limited stocks are maintained in the company's stores, items such as boots, ski bindings and ski poles have been part of the brand's product range since the beginning. Since the early 1980s, the company has developed even further and has become much more than just a ski brand. In just three generations, Stöckli has grown from a simple ski manufacturer to a sporting goods retailer offering a comprehensive range in the field of outdoor sports.

BICYCLE

In 1996 Stöckli introduced its first range of bikes. Based on highly significant experience gained in the field of competition, the bikes were designed in-house in the company's Research and Development unit. Every year the engineers design new models which are then assembled in Switzerland. The bike collection remains true to the brand's reputation. Thanks to their exceptional quality and top-of-the-range components, the bikes have quickly gained in popularity and have featured at the forefront of world competitions, as demonstrated by top Swiss biker Mathias Flückiger in the Cross-Country World Cup.

STROMER

The 3.0 bicycle

According to Bern legend, Thomas "Thömu" Binggeli, the founder of Stromer, sold the livestock of his parents' farm while they were on holiday, using the proceeds as seed money to launch his "Thömu" brand and open a bike shop. Shortly afterwards, the young visionary designed an incredibly innovative e-bike, the Stromer. In 2009 he filed patents and launched the first e-bike on the market.

The second Stromer model, the ST1, was introduced in 2011. This e-bike set new standards in elegance and in urban traffic performance. Thanks to its maximum speed of 45 km an hour with pedal-assist, it first enjoyed great popularity in Switzerland before going on to conquer the whole of Europe. And the "Rolls-Royce" of e-bikes has also gained notoriety in the United States. In the same year, Stromer was taken over by the Swiss premium bike brand BMC.

The firm, now established in Oberwangen near Bern, has lost none of its freshness. It continues to focus on innovation and deals exclusively with technology and style.

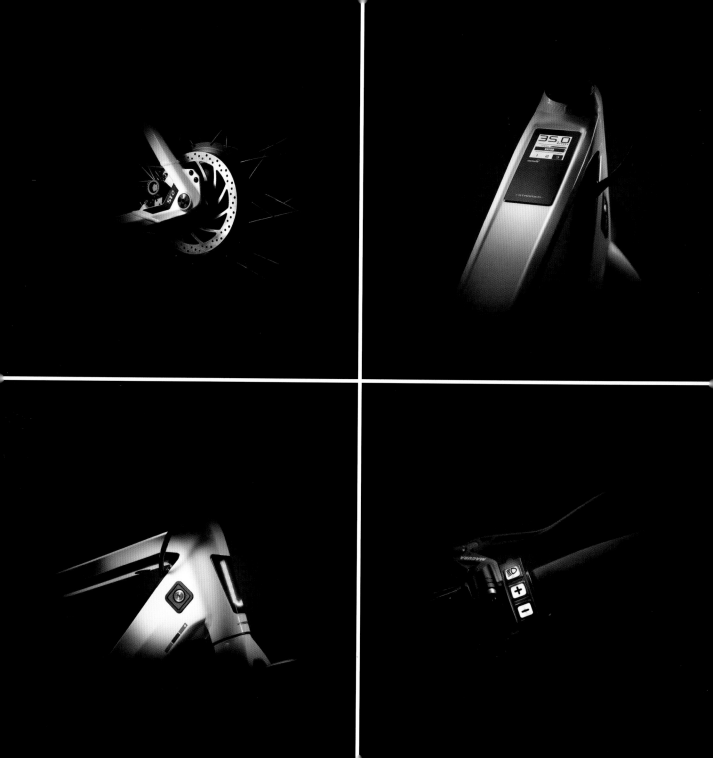

AN E-BIKE WITH DIGITAL NETWORKING

In March 2014, the brand once again hit the headlines with the ST2. Its S-Pedelec with pedal-assist was the first e-bike to boast digital connectivity. Omni, the ground-breaking new interface, combines the digital world of Stromer with the real world of the users. It is fully integrated and provides real-time telemetry data as well as having GSM, GPS and Bluetooth functions. Equipped with the latest digital technologies, the ST2 can communicate not only via Stromer's "Omni" App with its owner's smart phone but also receive instructions. The rider can use their smart phone to change their bike's settings at a distance and also activate the lock.

EXQUISITE EQUIPMENT

With two optional battery models and three motor types available, the Stromer boasts a continuous drive in the rear hub, which is controlled by the rider. The ST1 motor is available in three versions: the Mountain 25 for an easy ride, the Mountain 33 for endurance riding and the Power 48 for maximum speed.

Stromer bikes are equipped with hydraulic disc brakes and Schwalbe BigBen tyres. For optimum comfort, the lightweight carbon forks can be fitted with suspension.

The company's website now also offers customers a chance to choose the number of gears, the frame size, colour and position of the Stromer brand. A "women's version" for easier mounting, is also available.

TURNING PASSION INTO STYLE

Stromer bikes contain a certain contradiction, in that they blend extreme innovation and technology with uncompromisingly sober lines. The flawless design almost conceals the masterly prowess of the brilliant Swiss engineers. Utterly elegant, it combines a powerful motor with unprecedented autonomy. This structure, based on an exclusive underlying modular structure, and the technical developments are the result of uncompromising care and boundless passion that significantly impact every stage of development.

AN INSPIRATIONAL PHILOSOPHY

Appenzeller, Swisscom, PostAuto, BKW/FMB and many more have purchased Stromer e-bikes for their employees. Whether for reasons of sustainable development, the appeal of mobility or a healthy lifestyle, they have all opted for this new form of transportation and are justly proud of it. Fun (in innovation) is within reach!

A DURABLE, INNOVATIVE AND IMAGINATIVE MODEL

Whether before or after the acquisition by BMC — authenticity, innovation and passion have always been and remain fundamental Stromer values and find expression throughout the entire company, both internally and externally. It is therefore hardly surprising that the founder cites new technologies and major brands such as Tesla, Apple und Google as his sources of inspiration.

These days, the company's 4,400 m² head office at the foot of the Bernese Alps resembles a campus. The energy for the whole complex is insured by solar panels on the roof and all batteries used in the manufacture of Stromer e-bikes are charged with solar energy. The Oberwangen Campus houses management, design, development, installation, customer service and a Stromer Flagship Store under one roof. Silicon Valley, watch out!

Innovation is one of the main driving forces of the company, which handles all the essential manufacturing steps, from the development of mechanical and electrical components to the design of software and the integration of the complete system. In addition, Stromer is not only setting ground-breaking new standards in "traditional" bicycle technology, but also offering outstanding technological excellence and user experience. In virtuoso fashion, the versatile brand has built a bridge between urban sport and the world of geeks.

VICTORINOX

VICTORINOX
The stainless steel brand

Victorinox knives and multifunctional devices enjoy an outstanding reputation worldwide. It stands for Swiss quality, reliability, innovation and a pioneering spirit. In 1884, Karl Elsener founded a cutler's company in Ibach-Schwyz that would go on to become a global group. The brand name Victorinox is a neologism: a combination of the name of the founder's mother, Victoria, and 'Inox', the international designation for stainless steel. In the early years, Karl Elsener sought to combat poverty and unemployment in the Schwyz basin. He gave people jobs and prevented them from moving abroad. He founded the Association of Swiss Master Cutlers in a bid to establish domestic production of soldiers' knives. His efforts were rewarded as early as 1891 with the delivery of the first major consignment to the Swiss Army. And with that, Karl Elsener laid the foundation for a successful globally-oriented company. His sense of solidarity, local ties and strong belief in lasting values would also later influence the Victorinox corporate philosophy. Victorinox now operates in six business segments: pocket knives, household and professional knives, timepieces, travel gear, fashion and fragrances. Eight offices in Brazil, Chile, Hong Kong, India, Japan, the USA, Mexico and Poland fly the flag for the Victorinox brand throughout the world. The exclusive flagship and brand stores plunge customers into a world that blends tradition and innovation.

POCKET KNIVES / HOUSEHOLD AND PROFESSIONAL KNIVES

Victorinox pocket knives and multi-tools are popular throughout the world. The assortment comprises a range of over 400 models with up to 80 different functions. Recent outstanding developments include, for example, the prestige SwissChamp model with 33 functions or the Victorinox@work – a USB pocket knife with up to 32GB of storage capacity. New designs and limited editions – such as the Damast knives issued every year – appeal to the instincts of collectors. Victorinox offers about 650 different models of household and professional knives.

TIMEPIECES

Like the legendary Victorinox knives, the Victorinox Swiss Army watches embody the values and spirit of Victorinox – functionality, quality, innovation and iconic style. The collection includes around 150 Swiss-made timepieces, true high-precision instruments developed with longevity in mind and featuring a design that is as timeless as it is contemporary.

TRAVEL GEAR

The Victorinox Travel Gear collections offer a wide range of luggage: suitcases, lifestyle bags, rucksacks, travel accessories and personal leather goods. These products stand out above all for their quality and durability. The ultra-light and highly robust pure polycarbonate system is truly ground-breaking. "Best Buy" and "Best Luggage" are just two of the awards garnered from the travel experts.

FASHION

The Victorinox fashion collection for men and women offers ranges inspired by the seasons and made from natural materials and high-tech fabrics. Lightweight outerwear and underwear, knitwear and a variety of thermal basics bear the Victorinox signature. Their clear shapes and lines and daring designs in attractive colours are tailored to the active lifestyle of modern consumers. In developing the materials, Victorinox works with leading manufacturers from around the world.

FRAGRANCES

The Victorinox perfumers have managed to combine alpine freshness with the values of modern Switzerland to create a unique "Swiss feeling". The "Swiss Army" fragrance range plunges the wearer into a world of snow-capped mountains, majestic glaciers, lush green meadows and mountain lakes. The "Swiss Unlimited" collection is imbued with a sense of freedom and adventure. The distinctive, original bottles have received several awards, such as the Fifi Award amongst others.

FROM ARMY KNIFE
TO GLOBAL BRAND

1884 Karl Elsener opened a cutler's in Ibach-Schwyz.

1891 Elsener founded the Association of Swiss Master Cutlers. This enabled the first major delivery of soldiers' knives to the Swiss Army.

1909 After the death of his mother, who had always supported him with great enthusiasm, Karl Elsener paid tribute to her with the brand name "Victoria" and legally registered the emblem with the cross and shield. It is now registered in as a trademark in over 120 countries.

1921 The invention of stainless steel was of vital importance for the cutlery industry. Inox is the international designation for stainless steel. The current brand name "Victorinox" is a combination of "Victoria" and "Inox".

1931 The Brown Boveri company was awarded the contract to set up the world's first fully electric hardening plant in Ibach. The consistently high quality of all knives was thus assured.

1945 The "Swiss Army Knife" set out on a triumphant campaign to conquer the world. The U.S. soldiers stationed in Europe bought the knives in large quantities and took them home as popular souvenirs. The company quickly doubled its production capacity.

1989 Under the "Swiss Army Watch" brand, Victorinox and its U.S. partners at the time took the North American watch market by storm. A sales subsidiary in Japan soon followed.

1999 Victorinox luggage hit the international markets. Shortly thereafter, Victorinox launched a clothing line in the United States and opened the first Victorinox Store to feature the whole product range in Soho, New York.

2005 Victorinox took over Wenger SA, the traditional manufacturer of Swiss knives and watches in Delémont and continued to run the company as an independent subsidiary. Victorinox expanded still further as a global multi-brand.

2007 Foundation of the Victorinox "Swiss Army Fragrance AG". The former Wenger perfume line was repositioned as Victorinox fragrance.

2013 Victorinox incorporated Wenger knives in the Victorinox brand. The company employed over 1,800 employees and generated a turnover of about 500 million Swiss francs.

2014 Victorinox is now being managed by the fourth generation of the Elsener family. The company celebrates its 130th anniversary this year.

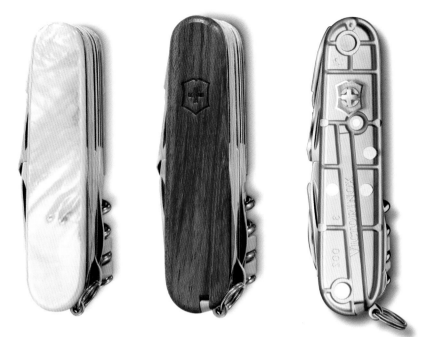

VICTORINOX SWISS CHAMP

33-function Swiss Army Knive (91 mm). Each knife is tested by hand for quality control. In many designs such as SilverTech, and as a unique model with high quality mother-of-pearl or wooden casing.

UNIQUENESS

Victorinox is a Swiss brand with tradition – and with a future. Quality, reliability and innovative strength are the core features of the products that have inspired people around the world. Victorinox is a brand built on solid traditional values, carried by creative specialists and managed by a sustainability and business-minded family. With this view for both the time-tested and new, the company upholds its brand promise to clients, employees and business partners in the long term. The family-run company looks back on a 130-year history and has maintained its independence and humanity. Cooperation in the large Victorinox family is characterized by mutual respect and trust. Carl Elsener, the fourth generation at the helm, works together with his siblings to manage the company. *"130 years of Victorinox is a major milestone for us and a great motivation to continue and further develop the life work of the Victorinox pioneers with just as much dedication."* Carl Elsener, CEO Victorinox

V-ZUG

Outstanding household electronics

The V-ZUG brand makes cutting-edge household technology. The ZUG-based company develops, produces and distributes high-quality electronic appliances. As the market leader in Switzerland for electrical appliances, V-ZUG can boast over 4.2 million appliances in service in its home country. Half of all Swiss households owns one of the brand's machines for cooking, washing, laundering or drying! The brand ascribes its leading position, which it vehemently defends, to its ability to adapt its products to the needs of its discerning customers, especially in terms of low fuel consumption, durability and careful use of natural resources. With the Premium Swiss Quality label, the brand has made a commitment to progress. Time and again it has developed inventions and innovations that set new standards of international significance.

Since its founding in 1913, the family-run business has become one of the biggest employers in the Canton of Zug. With its ultra-modern working methods and over 1400 highly qualified employees, the high-tech manufacturer has set itself a major challenge: to make everyday life easier.

A PIONEER WITH MORE THAN A CENTURY OF EXPERIENCE

For over a century V-ZUG has stood for high-quality household appliances. Founded in 1913 under the name Verzinkerei Zug AG as a jobbing galvanising company, the firm manufactured galvanised sheet metal products for the housing, agriculture and construction sectors. It scored its first major success in 1915 with the machines known as "Waschherden"; washing machines with water heated by fire. At the beginning of the 1920s, Verzinkerei Zug AG produced the first manually operated drum washing machine, which made housework easier still. Since then, the range has continued to expand. With the development of "Unica", the classic V-ZUG laundry room – consisting of a washing machine, washing tank, centrifuge and sink – was completed.

Shortly before 1950, the development of the first electric washing machine was a significant milestone from a technical point of view, because it saved people a great deal of time and energy. The brand continued to focus on innovation, witness for example the "Tempo" – the first small washing machine for the home – followed by the "Unimatic", the first Swiss automatic washing machine for multi-family houses.

The end of the 1970s saw the successful merger of the Zug metal goods factory, at the time the market leader for cookers and ovens, with Verzinkerei Zug AG. Production was based at what is now the head office, and the new company offered a full range of appliances for the kitchen and laundry room. From 1981,Verzinkerei Zug AG took on a new brand name: V-ZUG AG.

The following decades saw the company consolidate its leadership position with a range of innovative products and global innovations. Every product stood out for its technology or advanced design and new standards were set. The company conquered the market with a "green" washing machine, with tangible benefits in terms of energy saving and performance. Furthermore, V-ZUG is a leader in induction cooking in Swiss households, has developed new products for steam-cooking, entered into partnerships with top chefs and launched a dishwasher with "express" power, amongst other things.

INNOVATION FOR EVERYDAY LIFE

Throughout its 100-year history at the forefront of progress, V-ZUG has made a name with its pioneering inventions, world firsts, and design that offers a stylish combination of functionality and looks. Thanks to the many world innovations in various household domains, V-ZUG offers its customers an uncompromising practicality, based on highly advanced technologies. The "Premium Swiss Quality" label applies at all levels, in order to ensure the durability and reliability of the products. A proverbial quality that is entirely consistent with Zug's exceptional capacity for innovation.

SOME OF V-ZUG'S INVENTIONS ARE OF GLOBAL SIGNIFICANCE TO THIS DAY

1999 World's first limescale sensor.

2001 Electronic Steam System with external steam generator.

2004 World's first anti-crease steam and anti-mite programme.

2007 World's first Gourmet steam cooker.

2008 World's first WetClean V-ZUG.

2008 World's first Vibration Absorbing System (VAS).

2009 Fully automatic GarSensorik steam cooker

2012 First washing machine with heat pump technology.

2013 First dishwasher with heat pump technology.

RELIABILITY: THE HALLMARK OF V-ZUG

Great demands are made of equipment for the kitchen and laundry room – a cause to which the brand has been devoted for many generations. V-ZUG products are famous for their outstanding reliability, which is due in no small measure to components and values that have stood the test of time: quality, precision, innovation and customer orientation combined with Swiss engineering and know-how. Thanks to the robustness and durability of its products, the brand has won consumer trust: In the market study entitled EUROPEAN TRUSTED BRANDS, conducted by Reader's Digest at European level, the readers of «Reader's Digest Select» and «Reader's Digest Schweiz» were asked which brands they most spontaneously trusted. In the "Electronic household and kitchen appliances" product category, V-ZUG won the readers' vote in 2012 and 2013 for "MOST TRUSTED BRAND". Furthermore, the manufacturer also garnered the Pegasus Award 2013, which honours brands that are especially trusted by customers.

ELEGANCE AND DESIGN

Great demands are made of equipment for the kitchen and laundry room – a cause to which the brand has been devoted for many generations. V-ZUG products are famous for their outstanding reliability, which is due in no small measure to components and values that have stood the test of time: quality, precision, innovation and customer orientation combined with Swiss engineering and know-how. Thanks to the robustness and durability of its products, the brand has won consumer trust: In the market study entitled EUROPEAN TRUSTED BRANDS, conducted by Reader's Digest at European level, the readers of «Reader's Digest Select» and «Reader's Digest Schweiz» were asked which brands they most spontaneously trusted. In the "Electronic household and kitchen appliances" product category, V-ZUG won the readers' vote in 2012 and 2013 for "MOST TRUSTED BRAND". Furthermore, the manufacturer also garnered the Pegasus Award 2013, which honours brands that are especially trusted by customers.

UNCOMPROMISING AND FUTURE-ORIENTED

Durability and profitability, combined with the preservation of resources, have always played a key role in the V-ZUG AG philosophy – both in terms of appliances leading the way in low energy consumption and in the infrastructure of the company itself. In recent years, the company, which has long been ISO-14001 certified, has cut the energy consumption of its devices by more than half, thus proving its commitment to the environment. Furthermore, the Adora TSL WP heat pump dryer was voted the most environmentally friendly dryer in Europe ("Euro-TopTen" rating).

In Switzerland the company is the main business partner of the Minergie quality label. A further sign of the brand's commitment to the area of sustainable development is the monumental new V-ZUG logistics centre. Thanks to the latest energy achievements, it is virtually independent of external power sources. Ultra-modern solar cells and recuperation generators provide almost all the electricity consumed by the building.

PLUS X AWARD 2014 : PRIZES FOR FIVE V-ZUG PRODUCTS

The Plus X Award, launched over 10 years ago in Germany, is the most important international prize for innovative products. It is awarded to manufacturers who have made significant strides in quality and innovation, and recognises products that make life easier and more enjoyable or that are particularly environmentally friendly.

Product V-ZUG REFRESH-BUTLER Fabric care system.
Award Innovation, High quality, Functionality.

Product V-ZUG Adora SLQ WP Washing machine.
Award Innovation, High quality, Functionality, User-friendliness, Environmental friendliness.

Product V-ZUG Adora SL WP Dishwasher.
Award Innovation, High quality, Functionality, User-friendliness, Environmental friendliness.

Product GK46TIAKS/F/C Induction cooker.
Award High quality, User-friendliness.

Product Combi-Steam SL/XSL
Award Innovation, High quality, Functionality, User-friendliness.

APPENZELLER

The secret of mountain pastures

The homeland of Appenzeller cheese stretches between the Alpstein mountains and Lake Constance, in the north-east of Switzerland. A picturesque region punctuated by rolling hills, imposing mountains and lush meadows. It is here in this idyllic landscape, where centuries-old traditions survive to this day, that Appenzeller® cheese is made. For over 700 years Appenzeller® has been intertwined with the identity of the region.

CRAFTSMANSHIP

The way Appenzeller cheese is made is part of a heritage that has been passed down through generations. Twice a day, farmers bring freshly drawn milk to one of the 58 local dairies. Cheese makers then transform the milk into delicious Appenzeller® cheese. This process requires experience, diligence and a lot of manual labour. The cheeses mature in cellars over several months to reach their full flavour. The cheese makers turn the cheeses over regularly and treat them with a special herb-based brine. The brine penetrates the rind and gives the cheese its unparalleled flavour.

A UNIQUE TASTE

Appenzeller® cheese owes its success to a mysterious herb-based brine, which gives it its unique taste. The story of this magical mixture is a long one. This Swiss speciality was first documented in 1282. For a long time - since the Middle Ages - every cheese maker used his own herb brine. And of course, every cheese maker was certain that their recipe was the best. It was only at the beginning of the 1960s that Appenzell cheese makers agreed on a standard recipe for the herb brine. Since then, it has been made for all the dairies at the Emil Ebneter & Co distillery.

During the three to six month maturing period, each cheese is regularly rubbed with this special brine, which is how it acquires its flavour.

PRIORITISING QUALITY

In order to guarantee that only the very best cheese makes it to the shelves, the quality is rigorously controlled at every stage of production from field to dairy, including the cowsheds. When cheese merchants take possession of the cheeses, they carefully assess the quality. They evaluate the colour, the flavour and the holes.

The whole advertising campaign is like a saga that revolves around a humorous take on Appenzeller® cheese's big secret, the herb brine recipe. It always end up the same: with mute Appenzell cowherds.

The exact recipe for the herb brine is a secret that is guarded like prized treasure: only two people know the exact composition of the herb mixture. They are the only ones to have access to the safe where the recipe is kept under lock and key. The ingredients remain a secret, but here are a few clues: the special brine is a unique extract, taken from a mixture of more than 25 herbs, roots, leaves, flowers, seeds and peels using a complicated process.

To keep its secret, Appenzeller® cheese has had to renounce AOC or PDO certification. To obtain such a certification, the brine recipe would have to be divulged. However, the brand is still protected in Switzerland and abroad.

MAKING THE REGION'S ACTIVITIES SUSTAINABLE

So that future generations can also make a living from cheese making and to maintain Appenzell's natural paradise, the Sortenorganisation Appenzeller® Käse works to protect the area's countryside, people and traditions.

Making Appenzeller® cheese is a long process that involves different trades and often family-run farms. Expertise that is several centuries-old is passed down from generation to generation. The cheese is not produced on an industrial scale, it is made in collaboration with local dairies, giving them a way to secure their revenue in the long term. The organisation also divides up profits fairly, thereby supporting all those who participate in producing Appenzeller. An ethical practice that respects people, their trades and authenticity.

PRESERVING A HERITAGE

Sustainable development demands a long-term vision. One of the conditions for making Appenzeller® cheese is cattle farming that meets the animals' needs. Healthy, happy cows produce particularly good milk which has higher levels of nutritious proteins. Milk production is very important for Appenzell's countryside: grazing helps maintain the landscape.

FAVARGER

Chocolate manufacturer since 1826

In 1856, the daughter of the chocolate maker, Jacques Foulquier, married Jean-Samuel Favarger. The latter was working as watchmaker, but chose to learn the chocolate making profession together with his young fiancée under the guidance of Mr Foulquier. And so it was that the Favarger factory was founded. The chosen location was the île d'Oltramare, close to the mouth of the Rhône river, which provided it with hydraulic power. The first shop opened its doors a few months later at No. 5 Quai des Etuves (now named Quai des Bergues) and the company soon made a name for itself as one of the pioneers in the chocolate-making industry. Favarger is driven by a set of solid values, each of which is linked to the history and expertise of this almost two-hundred-year-old company.

Seven generations later, this intense passion for chocolate making is still very much alive. The founding family have always demonstrated an uncompromising commitment to the highest quality and to core human values, while remaining attached to the company's Genevan birthplace. And this connection is reciprocal: Aveline and Avelinette have been a part of children's snacks and indulgent moments for generations, becoming a veritable tradition akin to "Proust's madeleines" for Genevans.

Avelines: Favarger's star products.

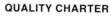

QUALITY CHARTER

The Favarger factory adheres to strict production standards and strives for quality in all its processes: sourcing of ingredients, roasting, grinding, conching, tempering, packaging and so on.

- 100% of the manufacturing processes are performed on-site, from selecting raw materials right through to finished product. Production is artisanal and semi-artisanal.
- Roasting and production of 100% of the masses of chocolate
- Chocolates contain 100% cocoa butter
- 100% Swiss-produced milk
- The aromas used are 100% natural
- 100% of Favarger products are Non-GMO certified
- The company's quality commitment is backed by several international certification bodies (pioneer of ISO 22000 certification in Switzerland)

THE FINEST RAW MATERIALS

Selecting and closely controlling the very best raw materials is the number one secret to achieving quality. The cocoa beans used in the blends determine the final quality of the chocolate. Each geographic area has its own taste. To create blends, Favarger combines the finest beans from South America and Africa. It also roasts 100% of the beans it uses. The natural origin and quality of all the raw materials guarantee the finest flavours. In addition to the cocoa beans, the company takes great care in selecting the ingredients that go into its recipes: ganaches and pralines are made using select Piedmont hazelnuts and Valencia almonds, Madagascan vanilla pods and honey from chestnut trees growing in the Piedmont hills. In addition, Favarger sources local Swiss products - milk, fresh cream, mountain flowers, spirits and brandies - from the very best suppliers with whom it has built relationships based on loyalty and trust.

FROM COCOA BEANS TO CHOCOLATE: THE MANUFACTURING PROCESS

The chocolate-making process requires great expertise and sophisticated machinery. Day-to-day activities at Favarger are driven by the values of excellence and ingenuity. The company performs all stages of the chocolate-making process from selecting raw materials to creating chocolate recipes. It roasts 100% of the beans it uses and manufactures 100% of the chocolates it sells. The chocolate-making industry is characterised by high levels of precision. Transforming beans into chocolate requires complex expertise which Favarger has cultivated with passion since 1826. Four major processes are undertaken in succession: roasting, grinding, conching/refining and tempering. At each stage, an understanding as well as a control of times and temperatures are crucial factors for obtaining the required quality and flavour. The temperature and length of time the beans are roasted is defined depending on the batches. This stage determines the quality of the chocolate. Control of this stage, which applies to the beans as well as to the hazelnuts and almonds, enables Favarger to produce blends freely according to the origin of the beans and its recipes. The key ingredients of the chocolate are mixed and ground. The powder is then emptied into

Favarger is the only remaining chocolate manufacturer in Geneva today. It is also one of the oldest Swiss chocolate makers which continues to roast cocoa beans and performs the entire chocolate manufacturing process. The company employs some forty staff, including master chocolatiers and craftspeople, and produces 260 tonnes of chocolate a year, which are sold in Switzerland and abroad.

mixers called "conches" which transform it, removing all unwanted substances and promoting the development of perfectly harmonious aromas. The temperature and duration of conching are specific to each recipe and give each product its signature taste.

SIGNATURE TASTE

Favarger boasts a legacy of some two hundred years of original recipes, which serve as a daily source of inspiration. Each of these tells a story, such as the exquisite Avelines invented in 1922, an iconic product which evokes memories for generations of lovers of quality chocolate.

Avelines / The Aveline recipe is one of Switzerland's most closely-guarded secrets. This praline encapsulates an exquisite fusion of chocolate and hazelnut - to which it owes its name. A selection of the finest raw materials and the experience of Favarger chocolate makers combine to bring out the true flavour of the ingredients: a soft, yet crunchy texture and an instantly recognisable taste.

The "Heritage" range / The recipes in the Heritage range have survived over the years to tell a unique story today. This chocolate is produced in a traditional way using time-honoured ingredients that recreate the special flavour and character of yesteryear. The chocolate makers use an age-old process of transforming the milk using a rolling mill to produce a uniquely flavoured paste with a delicate hint of caramel. This technique known as "rolling milk" is used in combination with raw cane sugar. During this process, the aromas of the beans and the mellow flavour of the milk are developed.

Fresh chocolates / All of the fresh chocolates are created from blocks of cocoa produced by Favarger. Pralines, ganaches, biscuits, Swiss-liqueur-filled sweets, truffles and chocolate-covered candied orange... Favarger's recipes have evolved thanks to the creativity of its chocolate makers and according to seasonal tastes. The praline remains faithful to the company's own special traditional recipe: ganache infused with vanilla, coffee or Earl Grey tea or blended with raspberry, passion fruit, Japanese yuzu and more...

FRESH CHOCOLATES

All of the fresh chocolates are created from blocks of cocoa produced by Favarger.

THE "HERITAGE" RANGE

The recipes in the Heritage range have survived over the years to tell a unique story today

FELDSCHLÖSSCHEN

The very best of Swiss beer

On 8 February 1876, the co-operate society «Kollektivgesellschaft Wüthrich & Roniger zum Feldschlösschen» brewed its first beer. The founder Mathias Wüthrich, a wealthy farmer, and Theophil Roniger, an experienced brewer, used only the finest quality hops and malt. Feldschlösschen soon came to be seen as the epitome of a tasty, high-quality beverage, as proved by the rapid growth in revenue and customer numbers – a success that was also due to the railway line that had been built the previous year between Basel and Zürich. The founding partners opted to transport their beer by rail – a modern and forward-thinking logical decision at a time when over 500 Swiss breweries continued to transport their beer every day by horse and cart. The expansion of Feldschlösschen was in line with the growth of rail transport across the nation. 22 years after the company was founded, production rose for the first time to over 100,000 hectolitres and Feldschlösschen became the largest brewery in Switzerland. After the death of the company founders, the breweries survived both World Wars, although the lack of the necessary ingredients and the resulting explosion in prices nearly brought sales to a complete standstill. In 1961, Max Wüthrich, the grandson of co-founder Mathias Wüthrich, took over the brewery and gave it a new impetus. 1974 saw a fundamental restructuring of the company, which began from

KEY DATES IN A STORY
OF RAPID GROWTH

1876 Foundation of Feldschlösschen brewery.
Production of 2,000 hectolitres in the first year.

1889 Direct connection to Rheinfelden station
by rail transport.

1898 Feldschlösschen becomes the leading
beer producer in Switzerland, with a production
of 100,000 hectolitres.

1905 Death of co-founder Mathias Wüthrich.

1913 Death of co-founder Theophil Roniger.

1961 Takeover of the company management
by Dr Max Wüthrich, grandson of co-founder
Mathias Wüthrich.

1970 Takeover of the Gurten AG Wabern company.

1972 Takeover of the Valaisanne brewery in Sion.

1974 Introduction of mineral and soda waters.

1989 Takeover of the Basel Warteck brewery.

1991 Takeover of the Freiburg's Cardinal brewery.

1996 Merger with the Hürlimann brewery.

1998 Takeover of the Rhäzüns mineral spring.

2000 Takeover of the Feldschlösschen drinks
company by Carlsberg Breweries of Denmark.

2009 Integration of the Kronenbourg and
1664 brands.

then on to also focus on the bottled water and soft drinks market. Feldschlösschen has taken over 36 breweries in its 135 year history. The company currently employs 1,300 staff and produces around 50 different drinks, including eight different varieties of beer, two mineral waters and the famous Schweppes brand, one of the world's oldest soft drinks. The company has a presence in 22 locations in Switzerland. For over a decade, it has been owned by the Danish Carlsberg Group and thus benefits from the network and dynamism of the world's fourth largest brewery group.

INGREDIENTS

The best ingredients, a high-quality manufacturing process and strict controls form the basis of the outstanding taste and high quality of Feldschlösschen beer. Brewing a good beer requires four ingredients: hops, malt, yeast and water.

In the production process, the brewers exclusively use female, unfertilised **hop flowers**, known as»Dolden«. They give the beer its slightly bitter taste and aroma of hops and increase its shelf-life as well as its foam strength.

In addition to hops, **malt** is one of the most important ingredients in beer making. During the malting process, barley is turned into malt. The addition of water enables the cereal to germinate and it is then dried at high temperatures. The colour, intensity and the taste of the beer – light or dark – is primarily dependent on the temperatures at which the malt is dried.

The alcoholic fermentation of the beer is achieved using **brewer's yeast**. With the help of enzymes, the sugar derived from the malt (maltose) is turned into alcohol and carbon dioxide.

Water constitutes 90% of beer and is an essential ingredient. The production of Feldschlösschen beer requires 1.2 million cubic litres of water per year.

Since the spring of 1989, it has been sourced from the from the depths of the Magdenertal in the Frick valley in Aargau. This mineral water is the best ingredient for obtaining a tasty beer.

BEER PRODUCTION

Although the techniques of beer production are constantly developing, the actual brewing process has remained unchanged for millennia. It still involves three steps: brewing, fermenting and storage.

Brewing / *Mashing:* The crushed malt is placed in a boiler (or mash tun) and mixed and heated with water to produce mash. The enzyme resulting from the malting of barley converts the malt starch into malt sugar (maltose).

Filtering / Once the mash has reached the desired temperature, the ingredients are separated into grains (dry) and wort (moist). The hops are mixed with the sweet wort and boiled. Various types of hops are used, depending on the beer variety.

Fermentation / The cooled wort is pumped into a boiler and fermented using brewer's yeast. The alcoholic fermentation process transforms the maltose into alcohol and carbon dioxide. Bottom-fermented beer requires around a week and must then continue to mature for a week in order to acquire its fine taste.

Maturation / The beer is then pumped into storage tanks so that it can further ferment for 1 to 2 weeks at low temperatures (approx. -2°C). The unwanted ingredients such as yeast and protein are deposited at the bottom. This clarification is important for the shelf-life of the beer. Finally, it is filtered, poured into casks, bottles or cans and transported to the point of sale.

INNOVATIONS

As a result of its experimental brewing techniques and the great expertise of the master brewer, the company has succeeded in producing new beers for the most demanding beer lovers. In recent years, Feldschlösschen has successfully brought a number of new products to market, including:

Feldschlösschen Amber / This beer matured on oak has an impressive fine bitter, spicy notes and a slightly caramel taste. The exclusive roasted barley malt gives it its bright amber colour.

Feldschlösschen Bügel / Is an amber-coloured lager, specially brewed for a flip-top bottle. It is the epitome of Swiss quality brewing.

Feldschlösschen Premium / Is Switzerland's leading premium lager. It matures at low temperatures and thus acquires a unique, full beer flavour with no bitter after-taste.

MÖVENPICK

Delicious ice creams created for gourmets

From the outset the Mövenpick brand has always been a symbol of culinary excellence. The group opened a number of fashionable restaurants between the end of the 1940s and the 1960s, before moving on to hotels. These establishments helped build its reputation for haute cuisine and outstanding service. The notion of service had such an importance for the brand that the management even took an innovative approach to its human resources policy. Employees worked fewer hours so they remained welcoming! Riding the wave of its success, the group also developed an ever-more refined cuisine (smoked salmon, wine, coffee, etc.). Between 1957 and 1958 the number of Mövenpick employees doubled from 300 to 600. An institution was born and with it, a premium brand with a considerable reputation. Mövenpick's first ice creams were developed in its restaurant kitchens at the end of the 1960s. Research and innovation are important cornerstones of the gastronomic tradition. In the 1970s, Mövenpick was one of the first companies to put a recipe with 'inclusions' (the addition of sauces or pieces) on the market. At first these ice creams were only available to diners at Mövenpick's restaurants, but they soon became widely available. Today almost 50% of Mövenpick ice creams are sold in the distribution sector and 50% are sold in high-end gourmet establishments.

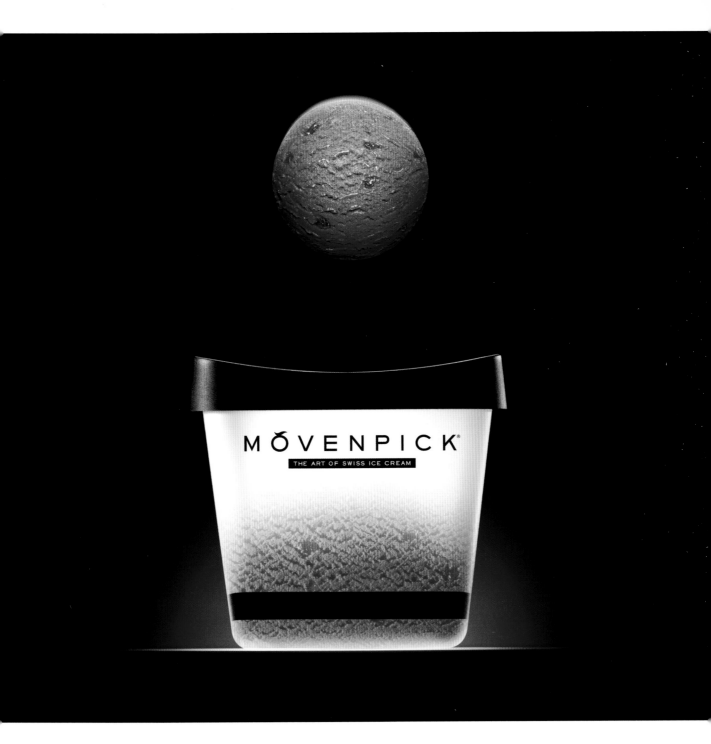

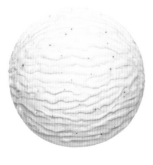

Mövenpick ice creams - which occupy a high-end niche - are sold in almost 40 countries in several thousand sales outlets in both western and eastern Europe, Russia, Middle East, Asia and in the central and southern Pacific areas. The brand is mainly focussed on Europe, where it has a strong presence: the brand is the Super Premium market leader in Switzerland and has a leading position in the gourmet market in the UK and in the "Take-Home Market" in Russia.

A PASSION FOR HAUTE CUISINE

The same initial, revolutionary vision of culinary excellence that gave rise to Mövenpick ice cream is still the brand's defining value today, and the same passion for haute cuisine is still driving its innovations. Mövenpick's Maîtres Glaciers are constantly looking for new tastes and textures, just as a great chef would do. Each recipe is the result of intelligent research and hard work, and provides the purest of pleasures. This means that Mövenpick is renowned for the sophistication of its recipes and the authenticity of its flavours. The ice cream's perfectly balanced flavours and inclusions of contrasting textures are defined by three elements: the selection of the best ingredients, unique expertise and the art of gourmet presentation and service.

DEMANDING THE BEST FROM NATURE

When creating a new product, Mövenpick starts by seeking out exceptional ingredients, which could take them to the farthest flung corners of the earth. Mövenpick's solid, lasting partnerships with its suppliers are essential to this quest for perfection: Mövenpick's unique supplier of La Gruyère double cream for its Double Cream & Meringue recipe is an authentic Swiss family-run dairy; its caramel is handmade in the Swiss region of Oberbaselbiet, which is famous for its traditional recipe. Only genuine Bourbon vanilla beans from Madagascar are used for its vanilla-based recipes. Its balsamic vinegar must come from Modena and original VSOP Cognac is used for its Cognac flavour... Each ingredient is selected from the best sources in the world in order to satisfy even the most demanding of gourmets.The company's expertise is embodied by a team of culinary specialist 'Maîtres Glaciers'. They are responsible for each recipe and their exacting standards can have an impact on every stage of the production process: from the selection of the ingredients to the way they are skilfully combined with Swiss ice

cream, not to mention manufacturing techniques. Mövenpick applies one fundamental rule throughout the creative process: 100% natural. No additives and no artificial colours or flavourings. All the flavours, textures and colours are derived exclusively from natural ingredients. This commitment is very unusual in the world of commercial ice cream production. The result is a level of refinement that no ordinary ingredient can rival.

PART OF THE NESTLÉ GROUP ELITE

Since 2003 Mövenpick Ice Cream has been run by Nestlé Worldwide Services SA, based in Vevey, Switzerland, and the brand is at the heart of the group's strategy for expansion into the global Super Premium sector. A natural choice given the brand's strong identity and its historic reputation for quality, which stems from the Swiss tradition of perfection. The principle: preserve the gastronomic traditions and prowess on which the brand's heritage is built, and bolster them through continually recruiting new culinary specialists in various disciplines - Maîtres Glaciers, confectioners, pastry chefs.

GOURMET COLLECTION

Sweet Dream / Classic combinations and refined flavours (Vanilla Dream, Strawberry, Maple Walnut, Espresso Croquant, Caramelita...)

Refreshing Dream / Harmony and simplicity with flavours such as Yogurt, Raspberry & Strawberry, Passion Fruit & Mango, Lemon & Lime, Apricot...

Endless Dream / A rich, creamy pleasure: White Chocolate, Tiramisu, Swiss Chocolate, Panna Cotta, Crème Brûlée, Cappuccino...

Surprising Dream / New flavours such as Rum Raisin.

"AT HOME" COLLECTION

Classics / Timeless flavours and famous desserts faithfully reinterpreted with ice cream. (Vanilla Dream, Caramelita, Tiramisù, Swiss Chocolate, White Chocolate, Strawberry, Stracciatella, Pistachio, Maple Walnut...)

Délices de Fruits / Sorbets made with real fruit. Fruity, refreshing flavours such as Raspberry & Strawberry, Passion Fruit & Mango, Lemon & Lime...

Limited Edition / Seasonal delights updated twice a year (Apricot & Rosemary, Coconut & Lemongrass, Kirsch & Cherry, Basler Läckerli...)

NESPRESSO

Pioneer turned gold standard

Since it began in 1986, *Nespresso* has redefined and revolutionised the way millions of people enjoy their coffee and has shaped the way we drink coffee at home. It all began with a simple idea: allow anyone to create the perfect cup of espresso just like a qualified barista. Inspired by Luigi Bezzera's original espresso concept, *Nespresso* developed a revolutionary system of aluminium capsules containing grinded coffee as well as machines that were specially designed for intuitive use. The *Nespresso* system aims to ensure a consistent level of quality and to provide a perfect cup of coffee at home.

Naturally, one of the fundamental aspects of this innovative idea was an unfaltering insistence on a high-quality raw material. Only 1% to 2% of the world coffee crop meets the quality, taste and aroma profiles required for the *Nespresso* Grands Crus. The coffee is then roasted and blended by the *Nespresso* coffee experts to create a variety of Grand Cru coffees to suit every taste. Today *Nespresso* offers more than twenty varieties for home enjoyment and nine for professionals. In addition, several limited editions are released every year. Each *Nespresso* capsule sold in the world is produced in one of the two state-of-the-art production sites in Switzerland.

Nespresso has an integrated research and development department, and now

produces a range of around 40 elegant, intelligent machines with the help of seven partners. Their design has been recognised with numerous prizes, including nine prestigious Red Dot Design Awards and two iF Product Design Awards.

The *Nespresso* system – the interplay of the genuine capsule with the coffee machine – soon made of the brand the coffee sector's gold standard and one of the world's most dynamic food and drink brands. *Nespresso* has a unique business model that helps it guarantee a high level of quality at every stage of the supply, production and sale of its coffee, and maintain an exclusive, close relationship with its clients.

Over 10 years of continuous innovation and investment have been necessary to make the brand financially viable after its creation. In parallel, it gained in amplitude as it moved into new markets. *Nespresso* later reached a double figure growth rate, confirming its success.

In less than 30 years, the company has made portioned coffee available to all. Today *Nespresso* operates in 60 countries and has more than 9,500 employees around the world, compared to 330 in 2000. In the markets, more than 70% of employees are in direct contact with consumers through more than 320 boutiques (compared with one in 2000) and customer relationship centres.

The brand is enjoying remarkable popularity: 50% of new members of its Club discovered *Nespresso* through their friends or family. More than 3.5 million fans like the brand on Facebook and 180,000 individual clients visit the online boutique each day.

The independent company is run on a global level by the Nestlé group. Its head office is in Lausanne, Switzerland.

COMMITMENT TO SUSTAINABLE GROWTH

Nespresso is committed long-term to integrating sustainability throughout its business operations, from coffee supply to recycling capsules, through carbon footprint reduction. The company has defined clear objectives and is looking to create shared value for the company itself and for society as a whole. The Ecolaboration™Program, launched in 2009, provides a global framework for managing partnerships, innovation and sustainable development. This philosophy is deeply rooted in the brand's business model and consists of three main points, the objectives for which have been reached at the end of 2013: put in place recycling systems to reach 75% of recycling capacity for used capsules (today there are more than 14,000 dedicated capsule collection points around the world); reducing the carbon footprint of each cup by 20%; and making sure that at least 80% of the coffee comes from the *Nespresso* AAA Sustainable Quality™ Program. This program, launched in 2003, represents a significant challenge: combining excellent coffee, productivity, social progress and environmental protection. The quality coffee is classified as AA in some countries, *Nespresso* has added a third A to signify new discerning criteria such as economic, environmental and social sustainability. The Program recently received proof of its beneficial impact on the lives of coffee growers, on preserving their environment and on the excellence of the coffee that *Nespresso* buys from them. An independent Colombian body, CRECE (the Centre for Regional Studies on Coffee and Entrepreneurship), studied 1,200 Colombian farms, both affiliated and non-affiliated with the AAA programme. On the three areas concerned, the difference in favour of the AAA farms was unquestionable. In 2013, more than 84% of *Nespresso* coffee was provided via this sustainable development programme. This success is down to the talents of 60,000 coffee growers.

Above: coffee berries, the roasting process, boutiques in Toronto, Saint Petersburg and the Nespresso (in italics) Cube in Barcelona airport.

30 YEARS OF REVOLUTIONISING COFFEE

Nespresso SA was founded under the aegis of the Nestlé group in 1986. During these pioneering years, the *Nespresso* system and its business model were constantly refined to improve consumer's coffee-drinking experience. *Nespresso* launched its first four varieties of Grand Cru: Capriccio, Cosi, Decaffeinato and Bolero (now known as Volluto), and proposed its first two machines (C100 and C1100), designed to resemble mini barista machines. The concept was first tested and launched in the office coffee sectors in Switzerland, Japan and Italy.

Three years later, in 1989, the system was introduced on the domestic Swiss market and the *Nespresso* Club was created in order to propose a range of exclusive, customised services for customers. It would become one the brand's defining features.

At this stage, growth was entirely based on consumers through 'sponsorship' offers.

1991 The company arrives in French and North American households, marking the first expansion phase. The first recycling programme for *Nespresso* capsules is set-up in Switzerland with 34 collection points. Two years later, capsule production capacity doubles in order to meet demand.

1995 *Nespresso* reaches break-even point. The first *Nespresso* machine designed for aviation is installed on Swissair, giving the brand first class exposure to international airlines.

1997 With *Nespresso* offering wider distribution, new partnerships are forged for the manufacture of its machines, with Jura for Switzerland, Magimix for France and Benelux, and KitchenAid in the United States.

1998 The website becomes an e-commerce platform meaning orders can be placed directly online 24/7.

1999 Launch of a new system designed for professional use: *Nespresso* Professional. Specialised machines and specially adapted coffee capsules are designed for SMEs and high-end restaurants.

2000 The first *Nespresso* boutique opens in Paris.

2001 The launch of the Concept machine with an ergonomic design, equipped with a new revolutionary 'open jaw' technology, which is easy to use and generates record sales.

2002 The capsule production capacity quadruples thanks to the first dedicated production centre in Orbe.

2003 The *Nespresso* AAA Sustainable Quality™ Program is launched in collaboration with the NGO Rainforest Alliance. It aims to promote high-quality 'sustainable' coffee production and supply.

2004 The first *Nespresso* boutique-bar opens in Munich. This new retail concept will later spread to New York and beyond.

2006 Nestlé Nespresso SA turnover exceeds 1 billion Swiss francs for the first time.

George Clooney becomes the brand's worldwide ambassador. He stars in the first series of advertising campaigns to feature celebrities.

2010 Nestlé Nespresso SA moves its international head office to Lausanne, in Switzerland, and exceeds 3 billion Swiss francs in turnover. The worldwide expansion accelerates with opening of new boutiques in major international cities. The 200th boutique opens in Shanghai, China.

2012 The opening of the first boutique-bar in San Francisco signals *Nespresso*'s US West Coast expansion.

2013 *Nespresso* launches *Nespresso* Cube, an entirely automated boutique. The brand thereby introduces a new shopping experience and rejuvenates personal service.

Machine *Nespresso*
Maestria Rosso.

OVOMALTINE

The most famous orange can in Switzerland

The name Ovomaltine is a byword for an extraordinary success story. It all began at the end of the 19th century in a laboratory in Berne's old town. The chemist Dr. Georg Wander was seeking a cure for malnutrition, which was widespread at the time. He chose to base it on a natural product that has been used for over 2,000 years for medicinal purposes and is obtained from germinated barley grains: malt. Using a special vacuum process, he developed a malt extract that served for decades as a life-saving tonic for infants and the sick. On his death, his son Albert took over the company. He was also a chemist and pharmacist and decided to improve on his father's formula, refining the product's taste and adding further natural and restorative ingredients. His idea remains the foundation for the original Ovomaltine recipe to this day: a mixture of sun-ripened barley, the basis for malt, along with eggs and milk, the first complete diet for young infants, is rounded off with a little cocoa, to produce a fine taste. The powder first marketed in 1904 was sold as a medicinal compound. But healthy and active people soon also discovered the invigorating effects of this revolutionary drink. Ovomaltine is a particular favourite of athletes. By 1906 the product had conquered the whole of Europe. From 1919 onwards, the Wander company was exporting worldwide and had conquered America, Asia and Africa. The drink can now be bought in over 100 countries.

Since 2002, Wander AG has belonged to the Associated British Foods Group, but retains its own management in Switzerland. "Our company works as an independent, medium-sized concern. We have local management structure and use our autonomy in order to continuously develop new products," says company CEO Arnold Furtwaengler. One of the main strengths of the company from Neuenegg near Berne, is its proximity to the market. "We listen to consumers and develop products that meet their needs. Just as Dr. Georg Wander did 150 years ago" adds Furtwaengler.

A PRODUCT LOVED BEYOND THE BORDERS

Today, the Ovomaltine brand is closely associated with Switzerland. Whether for breakfast, during a break, while exercising or on the ski slopes, Ovomaltine is constantly developing its range. Alongside the powder in the orange can the range now includes several more products such as ovo drink, muesli, bread spread, chocolate and biscuits. The products are available almost everywhere, primarily in supermarkets, but also in restaurants, cafés, kiosks and petrol stations.

Ovomaltine is known to 99% of all Swiss people! This dynamic brand lies close to the top of the popularity rankings . The market study "BrandAssetTM Valuator 2013" by the Y&R Group found that it was among the 20 most popular brands in Switzerland. For 18 to 29-year-olds, it even figures amongst the top ten!

Energy and stamina, combined with a positive mental attitude, are values closely associated with Ovomaltine and its advertising. The slogan "With Ovomaltine, you can't do it better, but longer." has been used by the brand since 1998.

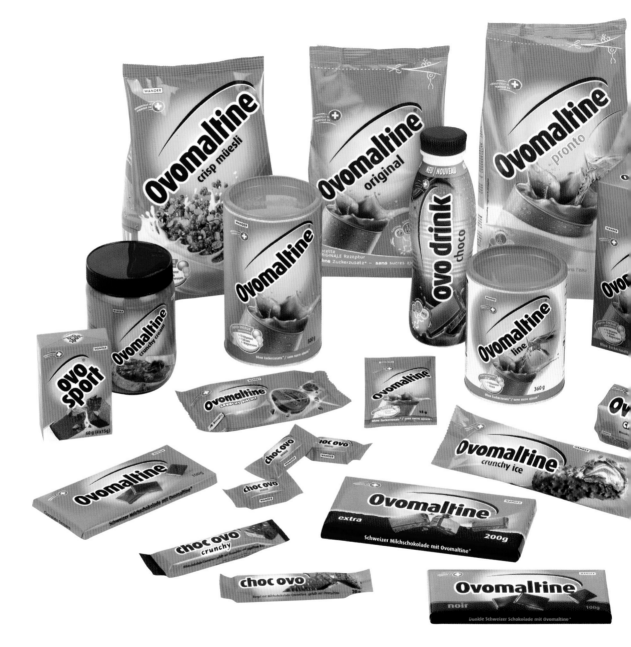

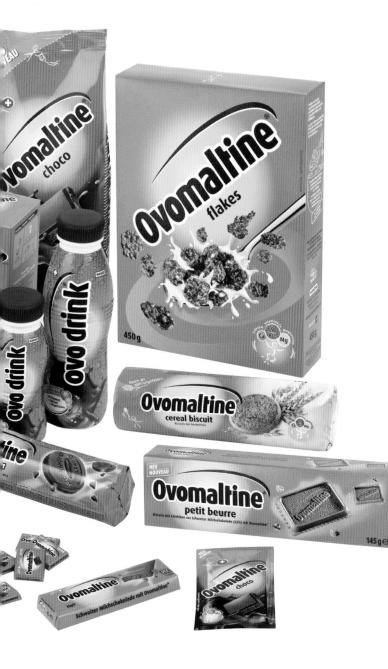

HISTORY

Innovations play a central role in the story of Ovomaltine – whether in sponsoring events, product development or in advertising. A few examples:

1920's Wander offered a catering service for the first time at a sports competition on the grounds of Berne University and thus became a pioneer in sponsoring.

1937 With the introduction of ovo sport, the company launched the first convenience product in 1937. The bar was initially used as food during military service. Active people and athletes later discovered it for themselves.

1967 Swiss television was still in its infancy. Wander was one of the first Swiss companies to make TV advertising.

1988 The slogan "With Ovomaltine, you can't do better, but longer." was first used.

2005 The Ovomaltine crunchy cream spread conquered the Swiss breakfast table.

2015 Wander AG celebrates its 150th anniversary.

AN ALLY OF ACTIVE PEOPLE EVERYWHERE

Ovomaltine and sport have long been an inseparable partnership. The energy brand has already partnered the Olympic Games, cycle races such as the Tour de Suisse, gymnastics events, skiing competitions and football World Cups.

In 1932, Wander was responsible for the catering for athletes and officials at the Olympic summer and winter games for the first time. The brand went on to service a further 19 Olympic Games until 1976.

In 1972, Ovomaltine launched the famous "Ovo Grand Prix", which for 25 years was one of the biggest events in skiing. Many Swiss skiing stars began their careers in the competition, including Pirmin Zurbriggen, Erika Hess and Didier Cuche.

Didier Cuche and Ovomaltine: an enduring partnership.

The cooperation between Didier Cuche and Ovomaltine began in 1998 after the Olympic Games in Nagano. Since then, the skier from Neuchâtel has always set off from the starting line in an orange helmet. Ovomaltine has been part of the athlete's life since his childhood. As a young man, he gained experience in the Ovo Grand Prix. He later proved himself with impressive performances at the World Championships. Cuche's great ambition and talent led him to the pinnacle of Swiss skiing, and his friendly, down-to-earth and open manner made him the perfect ambassador. He has remained in action on behalf of Ovomaltine even after his retirement.

The twelve brands of Wander.

modifast®

WANDER

viomalt
Malzextrakt

Caotina®

jemalt®

Ricola

RICOLA

The secret is Chrüterchraft

Ricola was founded by Emil Richterich in 1930 and the family business is now being run by the third generation. Having developed a magic blend of 13 herbs from the Swiss mountains for the production of sweets, ten years later the baker laid the foundation for his company's success. Thanks to the recipe, and the distinctive features and values of the brand, the company now enjoys worldwide success.

The original recipe has remained unchanged for over 70 years. It also forms the basis for the Ricola products. The range today includes over 40 varieties of herbal sweets and tea specialities, which come in a variety of packaging. Around 290 million boxes leave the production plant every year. Around 90% of these are exported to over 50 countries, from Europe to the Middle East and from Asia to the USA and Latin America.

According to Biscosuisse, the Swiss Baking and Confectionery Industry Association, around 70% of all Swiss sweets are made by Ricola.

Swiss tradition, coupled with an innovative spirit, has turned Ricola into a company with a worldwide presence, whose name stands for natural herbal specialities on every continent. The continued success of Ricola is based on the hard work of its employees and their distinct sense of quality.

HISTORY

1930 In his home village of Laufen, the baker Emil Richterich founds the Richterich & Compagnie Laufen Factory, and the name "Ricola" is born out of the first two letters of each word– but not until 1967.

1940 He invents the carefully guarded recipe for Ricola Swiss herbal sweets, based on 13 herbs.

1960s Ricola exports to Italy, Luxembourg, Germany and France. Annual turnover amounts to 1.3 million Swiss francs.

1970s The brand expands its international presence and exports to the USA and Asia, via Japan, Hong Kong and Singapore.

Emil Richterich, the company founder, dies in 1973. His sons Hans Peter and Alfred take over the company management.

1983 With its contractually agreed purchase of herbs, Ricola contributes to the promotion of herb cultivation in the mountain area and to the foundation of the Association of Swiss Herb Producers.

1987 Founding of Ricola USA, Inc. in Morris Plains, New Jersey.

1991 Felix Richterich leads the family concern into the third generation.

1993 The creation of the famous Ricola cry, which would soon go on to be known around the world

1994 Founding of Ricola Asia Pacific Pte Ltd. in Singapore.

2006 Founding of the daughter company Divita S.r.l. in Italy and Ricola (Asia-Pacific) Limited in Hong Kong

2007 Ricola's turnover exceeds 300 million Swiss francs for the first time.

Ricola now employs around 400 staff, including 370 in Switzerland.

SOCIAL RESPONSIBILITY

Alongside its commitment to upholding cultural values and the support of charitable projects, Ricola is also aware of its responsibility both as a major employer in the region and to its herb producers. Over 100 independent farms from Valais, Jura, Emmental, Poschiavo and Central Switzerland have signed contracts with Ricola. The cultivation of herbs for Ricola constitutes an important income supplement for most of these farming families. Ricola enters into multi-year customer contracts with its suppliers in recognition of their fairness and reliability as business partners.

CATCHY ADVERTISING CAMPAIGNS

"Riiiiicolaa!" This cry is closely associated with the brand around the world. A 1993 television advertisement featured two farmers shouting "Riiiiicolaa!" at each other. The advert met with such success in Switzerland and Germany that Ricola decided to include the Ricola cry in adverts in other countries.

No Ricola advert since 1993 has been without the famous cry. What began as a simple act in a TV advert has reached international cult status in under 20 years.

"Who invented them?" A small and dashing employee travels from one country to another to tell tall tales about the invention of Ricola sweets. With this advertising strategy, the brand has managed to communicate its basic values in a unique and humorous way: Switzerland, herbs, effectiveness and enjoyment.

The new global Chrüterchraft campaign / In its latest global brand campaign, Ricola goes a step further and reveals exactly what the traditional Swiss company has invented: "Chrüterchraft". Chrüterchraft – A magical word with 13 letters for a sweet containing 13 herbs. Chrüterchraft is a Swiss word that stands for herbs, effectiveness and enjoyment. This one word contains all the Ricola values: a magical blend of herbs, coupled with the Swiss origin, effectiveness and taste of the sweets. The campaign has been rolled out worldwide since 2013.

The original recipe has remained unchanged for over 70 years. It also forms the basis for all Ricola products. The range today includes over 40 varieties of herbal sweets and tea specialities, which come in a variety of packaging.

ORGANIC CULTIVATION

For over 30 years, Ricola has been committed to growing herbs naturally in Switzerland, totally forgoing the use of pesticides, herbicides and fungicides – an area in which the company has set new pioneering standards. All Ricola farmers grow their herbs in accordance with the norms of organic farming – a philosophy that not only supplies Ricola with top quality herbs for processing, but also preserves the biodiversity of Switzerland.

THE 13 MAGIC RICOLA HERBS

Horehound activates the immune system, eliminates contaminants and protects the respiratory tract from dust particles. The bitter substances also protect the liver, thereby optimising the digestion and elimination processes. They strengthen excretion via the kidneys and therefore activate them.

Burnet has an anti-inflammatory, expectorant, soothing, invigorating and revitalising effect that stimulates the immune system. It is good for catarrh of the upper respiratory tract. It heals the trachea and soothes bronchitis, asthma, coughs, sore throats and hoarseness, strengthening the body's own immune system, prophylaxis and treatment of influenza.

Speedwell has a number of beneficial effects: The active ingredient Aucubin frees the body from burdensome infectious agents, the tannins seal the mucous membranes and the bitter substances tighten the pores, resulting in a healthy complexion. Speedwell relieves inflammation in the digestive tract and optimises food intake. It also acts as a blood purifier.

Marshmallow is valued above all for its soothing essential oils. It creates a protective film on mucous membrane under attack, regenerating and moisturising dry throats.

Lady's Mantle balances hormonal fluctuations in women, especially during puberty and menopause. During this time of radical change in women's bodies, the herb can be used as a tonic for all the female organs. Lady's Mantle helps women focus on their primordial power and encourages all people to become more aware of their intuition.

Elder really has it all. For example, the flavonoids rutin, isoquercitrin, quercitrin and hyperoside as well as essential oils, mucilage and caffeic acid derivatives. The fruits have antioxidant and antiviral properties. The fruit acids contain vitamin C and folic acid. Elder is thus used, amongst other things, for the treatment of colds and feverish catarrhs of the respiratory tract. It induces sweating and thereby reduces fever. It increases bronchial secretions and modulates immune responses.

Mallow helps mucous membranes in the mouth and throat, dry coughs, gastritis and dyspepsia.

Peppermint has particular healing powers. Its strengths include cooling inflamed mucous membrane and promoting blood circulation. It acts against infectious agents and expels them quickly from the body. Its tannins seal cracked mucous membrane, its bitter substances restore vigour and its flavonoids keep blood vessels flexible and stable. It cools hot heads and soothes stomach burn and can also regenerate inflamed digestive tracts.

Sage, or its essential oil, cleans the mouth and throat of infectious agents, its tannins prevent excessive perspiration and its bitter substances strengthen the digestive tract and eliminate bad breath.

Yarrow can be used for internal and external wounds. The herb has antibacterial, anticonvulsant and anti-inflammatory properties. Agents with active yarrow ingredients can help combat convulsive disorders of the stomach and intestinal area or menstrual cramps. Because it stimulates the digestive juices, it also helps ward off loss of appetite.

Cowslip helps cure the effects of the winter cold. Whether suffering from a stubborn cold or aching limbs from low body temperature, cowslip is an expectorant, warms the body and enables the head and chest to breathe properly again. It also is used to treat gout, rheumatism, heart weakness and dizziness. Its detoxifying effect should also not be overlooked: it acts a diuretic and sudorific and is therefore well suited for purifying treatments.

Plantain helps with scratches, abrasions, insect bites, burns and rashes. It works primarily on the respiratory tract as a cleaning agent. Its mucilage soothes a rough or inflamed mouth and throat and it soothes coughs and acts as an expectorant. It also works to reduce irritation in catarrh of the upper respiratory tract.

Thyme, or the active ingredients contained in its essential oil, can neutralise toxins. Its bitter substances act to tense the muscles, arousing strength and courage according to legend. The tannins also seal injured mucous membranes – so that no strength is lost.

TOBLERONE

A taste of Switzerland for all corners of the world

Jean Tobler began working at the Küntz confectionery in 1867. He took over the family business after the confectioner's son died due to illness. Tobler moved his "Confiserie Spéciale" into the first floor of a new building a few months later. In 1899, there was so much demand for his chocolate that he decided to open his own chocolate factory, founding Tobler & Cie. in Bern together with his sons. At the beginning, the chocolate products of this boutique confectionery were made using pre-produced products obtained from other well-known manufacturers such as Rudolf Lindt and Philippe Suchard. Then, on 26 February 1900, the company Berner Chocolaterie J. Tobler was entered in the commercial register. After the retirement of Jean Tobler, his son, 24-year-old Theodor Tobler, took over the management of the company. Theodor Tobler and Emil Baumann (his cousin and production manager) invented the Toblerone in 1908. The name is a fusion between Tobler and "Torrone", the Italian word for nougat with honey and almonds. Emil Baumann discovered nougat after travelling to France at the start of the summer to find out more about confectionery production. Upon his return to Switzerland, he shared his discovery with his business partner and suggested they try combining this "new" form of confectionery with milk chocolate. Theodor Tobler was immediately enthusiastic about this very promising idea,

SOME IMPORTANT DATES

1899 The Tobler chocolate factory is founded in Bern.

1908 The very first Toblerones are produced.

1909 The Toblerone recipe is patented.

1941 Theodor Tobler dies in Bern.

1947 Aer Rianta opens the first duty free shops in the Irish town of Shannon.

1963 Toblerone is exported from Bern to 101 countries.

1964 Participation at the World's Fair in New York.

1968 Toblerone is portrayed as a symbol of Switzerland In the James Bond "On Her Majesty's Secret Service".

1969 The dark chocolate Toblerone is launched.

1970 Suchard and Tobler merge to become Interfood; Tobler remains purely a production company.

1972 Multifood Ltd. is founded, and exports Tobler and Suchard products to more than 110 countries.

1973 The white chocolate Toblerone is launched.

1982 Interfood is taken over by Joh. Jacobs Co. GmbH and the name is changed to Jacobs Suchard.

1985 Production commences in Bern-Brünnen.

1990 Philip Morris acquires Jacobs Suchard and integrates the company into its new Kraft food division.

1991 The production of Toblerone is centralised in Bern-Brünnen.

1993 Kraft General Foods and Jacobs Suchard merge into a new food company at European level.

1994 The triangular Toblerone shape is now also trademark-protected alongside the name and packaging.

2000 Kraft Jacobs Suchard becomes Kraft Foods.

2008 Toblerone celebrates its 100th anniversary.

2012 Kraft Foods is divided into the Kraft Foods Group and Mondelez International, to which Toblerone belongs.

Toblerone products today, 2014.

and the duo wasted no time, getting down to work that very same evening in Theodor's private kitchen. After numerous attempts, they eventually managed to make the world's first chocolate bar, the milk chocolate Tobler with almonds and honey nougat. They patented the recipe on 29th March 1909. To this day, Toblerone chocolate remains simply unmistakable. It consists primarily of Swiss chocolate as well as nougat, which is made from honey, almonds and egg white. The chocolate bar, which takes the form of a row of small isosceles triangles, comes in different varieties. Toblerone is available in 120 countries and in many duty free shops. But the brand's success is down to much more than just the product's ingredients. Since its birth at the start of the 20th century, the company's philosophy has been based on four pillars: product quality to satisfy the customer; advertising to generate awareness; sales channel expansion to sell the chocolate abroad, not just in Switzerland; and a competitive price. Even after more than a hundred years, these principles remain an essential part of the Toblerone strategy.

PIONEER OF "SWISSNESS"

In 1916, at the suggestion of the board of directors, Tobler began using powdered milk in its chocolate. Soon after, it established its own dairy farm at the Alpine foothills in Schwarzburg, which supplies the headquarters in Bern with the required amount of powered Alpine milk each day. Toblerone is therefore a product made from Swiss raw materials.

Original Toblerone in 1908.

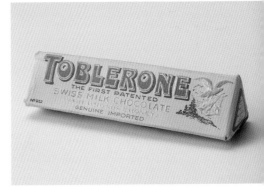

STILL JUST A SINGLE PRODUCTION PLANT

For a brand like Toblerone which is available worldwide – around 96 percent of the products are exported – consistent quality is of utmost importance. Consumers around the world quite rightly expect chocolate that has been produced in accordance with the highest quality standards and the rules of Swiss chocolate production. It has to taste the same everywhere. That is why, even after all these years, Toblerone – from the cocoa bean to the finished chocolate – is still produced in a single location, the factory in Bern-Brünnen. Each year, around 220 highly qualified staff (including trainee food practitioners) from some 20 different countries process 345 wagons full of sugar, as well as milk from around 14,000 Swiss dairy cows spread across 680 farms of various sizes. Three different cocoa masses are created for milk chocolate, white and

dark chocolate, which are then sold as the finished product in various sizes ranging from 6 g to 4.5 kg. The cash cow of this traditional Bern-based company, which enjoys an excellent reputation among the population, is the milk chocolate Toblerone, which accounts for 75 percent of sales. The unmistakable Toblerone advertising images portray Switzerland as a land of mountains. One symbol of Switzerland is the Matterhorn, which was pictured on the packaging from 1970 to 1987. It was then portrayed in blue and white stylised form before being replaced again with a picture of the mountain in the year 2000. It has remained the same since. What most people don't notice: A shiny bear can be seen standing upright in the middle of the mountain. This is a reference to Bern, where Toblerone is produced.

INITIATIVES WITH GREAT FORESIGHT

In the 1920s, Chocolat Tobler added a literary office to its communication department. The Tobler Journal – a twice-monthly magazine for Tobler chocolate sellers – was based in this new unit between 1920 and 1926. The aim of the magazine was to strengthen the relationship between the brand and the bakers and general stores, in order to boost the sales of Tobler products. The Tobler Journal covered different topics such as shop window decorations. The brand mastered the art of sales at a very early stage. After the Second World War, it used the emerging method of air transportation – especially for long distances – to grow the business and secure a permanent position in the duty free shops at airports. This strategic location is particularly important in self-service, as every transatlantic flight has to stop off to restock and refuel.

TOWARDS A SUSTAINABLE FUTURE

As well as adhering to the highest quality standards in the area of production, the company has started focusing more on sustainable development over the past eleven years. Between 2002 and 2013, its total energy consumption fell by 58 percent and its water consumption by 76 percent. What's more, the most important ingredients, such as cocoa beans and sugar, are delivered by rail, and 35 percent of the products are loaded onto the trains at the production plant in Bern and shipped directly from there. In addition to offering economic advantages, these measures also promote sustainable development on a global level.

VALSER ⊞

VALSER

Pure Swiss Alpine Springs

Valser natural products, sourced from an ecologically unspoilt environment, can lay claim to the very finest quality. Valser Classic and Naturelle have flowed for 25 years through several layers of rock before bursting naturally forth from St Peter's Spring in the Vals Valley. Following this decades-long process in the depths of the rocks, the factory produces the pure, crystal clear Valser mineral water, enriched with precious minerals, straight from the spring. Valser Silence bubbles up to the surface at St Paul's Spring after 3 to 5 years from a depth of around 100 m, at 1,806 m above sea level. Its low mineralisation gives Valser Silence a pleasantly smooth taste. In order to preserve this treasure long into the future, the company's activities are driven by a sense of responsibility towards the environment in general and to the Vals Valley and its inhabitants in particular. The mineral springs of Vals play a key role in the region. With around 80 employees, the company is one of the most important employers in the region.

GEOLOGICALLY UNIQUE SPRINGS

Long before Valser mineral water was available in bottles, it was used for bathing. In fact, natural mineral water was used even earlier both for internal and external purposes. St Peter's Spring was first mentioned by name in 1622. The success story

of Valser mineral springs began in 1960, when the entrepreneurs Hess and Schrauder discovered St Peter's Spring and bottled the precious natural mineral water. From 1961, the highly popular "Valser Man" could be seen travelling from house to house to sell his wares – a service which continues to this today.

St Peter's Spring

It takes the purified and balanced Valser Classic and Naturelle 25 years to bubble up fresh from a depth of 1000 m, in the Piz Aul mountains (3,121 m) in the primaeval valley of Vals in the heart of the Bündner Alps in Switzerland. A natural recipe that's a million years old.

St Paul's Spring

Our proprietary Swiss Alpine spring at an altitude of 1,806 m – one of the highest springs in Europe, situated in the Piz Aul (3,121 m) mountain range There, up in the heights, the pure, fresh and crystal clear Valser Silence springs forth with its pleasant, gentle taste.

AN ELIXIR FOR LIFE

Our bodies consist of 60 to 80 per cent water – in order to function properly, they need one and a half to two litres of fluid per day. Valser Classic and Naturelle are among the natural mineral waters with the highest mineral content. Natural mineral water offers your body optimum protection against the stresses, strains and harmful effects of modern life.

UN SUCCÈS CONTEMPORAIN

1960's The German investor Kurt Vorlop begins to tap the St Peter Spring and sells the brand soon after to Donald Hess. The water is initially marketed as "Vals" and sold by the Hess Group. In 61, VALSER is bottled at the Adula premises and sold by the "VALSER Service" home delivery company. First deliveries to shops in 66.

1968 Construction of the first major bottling plant at today's Boda site.

1970 First VALSER advert on Swiss television.

1983 VALSER launches in the gastronomic sector.

1984 Launch of VALSER Naturelle, complementing the sparkling VALSER Classic.

1985 VALSER expands northwards and exports to Germany for the first time.

1990 Launch of LIMELITE cool lemon water – one of the first flavoured mineral waters, in a glass bottle designed by Luigi Colani.

2001 Mario Botta creates "La Bottiglia" for VALSER in PET bottles.

2002 Takeover of VALSER Mineralquellen SA by Coca-Cola.

2003 In addition to VALSER Classic, VALSER Naturelle also becomes available in PET bottles.

2004 VALSER is exported to Russia.

2005 Launch of VALSER Viva in three flavours: Pear and Balm, Lemon and Herbs, Lime and Lemongrass.

2007 The first VALSER bottles are exported to Eastern Europe and Japan.

2010 Launch of Valser Silence from the new St Paul Spring.

"The Source" designer
bottle with Sports Cap.
Valser Classic.

"WATER IS MORE THAN JUST WATER"

The author and sommelier Arno Steguweit tastes mineral waters from around the world with the same love with which he tries his wines or champagnes in his everyday role. His tasting notes on Valser water read as follows...

VALSER SILENCE

"This natural still mineral water is very pleasant and gentle. A great accompaniment for meals, with a soft and mild taste. I recommend it with long dinners - it refreshes and cleanses the palate between courses to perfection. Its subtle mineralisation has made it extremely popular.

VALSER CLASSIC

"I recommend it to go with rich flavours and intense wines. Its pleasantly low of carbon dioxide content is refreshing, creating a wholesome effect, as if revitalised by nature. A balanced mineralised, highly distinctive and characterful mineral water."

VALSER NATURELLE

"Highly mineralised, full-bodied, meaty and polarising, but also refreshing. The calcium content gives it a fresh taste."

XELLENT

Excellent Swiss distillates

The tradition of distillation in the Willisau village dates back to the year 1918. Back then, aged just 20, Hans Affentranger founded a company producing spirits, liquors and syrups. His products rapidly gained in notoriety and fame, well beyond the confines of the region. The fruit liquors produced by the family business were a particular hit in restaurants and at celebrations. That liquor laid the foundation for today's DIWISA distillery, built on a family tradition stretching back almost 100 years. As in times past, the distilled spirits are still produced using traditional methods in copper tuns in a perfect blend of ancestral craftsmanship. Innovation and high-tech equipment. DIWISA is not only a market leader in Switzerland, but also counts as one of the most modern distilleries in Europe. since 2005, it is also been successfully producing alcohol-free drinks for the lifestyle and wholefood markets. The company is ISO and FSSC 22000 (Food Safety Standard) certified.

DIWISA currently employs one hundred staff and generates annual sales of CHF 145 million in 32 countries. The designation "Spirit of the year 2013/2014" is a testament to the outstanding quality of its products.

Its main focus is on building a successful brand at home and abroad. The company's TROJKA product is the strongest and most innovative spirit brand in Switzerland.

RAW MATERIALS FROM THE HEART OF SWITZERLAND

The raw materials used in XELLENT spirits are exclusively natural ingredients that are primarily sourced from the heart of Switzerland. They give the excellent distillates their character: rye from the fields and fine herbs, flowers and berries from the forest and garden. A perfect balance between the flavours is ensured by the soft fresh glacier water from Mount Titlis, which is particularly rich in minerals.

Rye from the Napfbergland / The most important raw material after the glacier water is provided by the highest quality Swiss rye varieties known as "Picasso" and "Matador". These are grown in natural surroundings on small farms in the Napfbergland. The fields, which are situated at a height of 500 to 800 m, are no bigger than 2 acres and belong to 18 different farmers. These cereal growing areas are located in central Switzerland, at the foothills of Mount Napf.

Herbs, berries and flowers from Switzerland / Edelweiss is planted on farms, according to organic regulations. However, the lemon balm and lavender are planted by the Master Distiller in the company's own garden. He finds an abundance of woodruff and elderflower during his long walks through the woods near Willisau. The recipe is rounded out with other herbs, the details of which are a well-kept secret!

Glacier water / The glacier water comes from Mount Titlis in the heart of Switzerland. It meanders its way down the mountain range and into the Engelberg Valley from a height of 3,000 m, where it is drawn from a depth of 30 m. This millennia-old crystal clear water, rich in oxygen and mineral content, gives the vodka it's incomparable taste. Furthermore, as a result, XELLENT is nearly pH neutral, unlike other spirits.

AN OUTSTANDING VODKA IN 6 STEPS

The rye processing / The fields are regularly visited in order to determine the perfect timing for the rye harvest. After the corn is harvested in dry weather at the end of the summer, it is transported to the small country mill located just a few hundred metres from DIWISA. There, the grains are cleaned and crushed before being used to produce XELLENT. Their quantity is limited, but their quality is all the higher.

First distillation / In the first distillation, the fermented rye mash is roasted in traditional small 500-litre copper tuns to produce the first distillate with an alcohol content of 72%.

The company's TROJKA product is the strongest and most innovative spirit brand in Switzerland.

This unusual method is thought to be the most gentle, because it does not allow for overheating.

Further processing / In three stages, the strength of the ground rye is macerated, liquefied, sugared and gently fermented. At each stage, a quality check is carried out.

Second distillation / In the second distillation, the raw distillate is treated in a copper column with 45 bubble trays and gently condensed. DIWISA is the only distillery in Switzerland to boast such a facility and thus be able to produce an excellent distillate of this quality.

Third distillation / In the third distillation, the final remaining unwanted ingredients are removed and once again refined and harmonised. The quality is monitored using the latest analytical equipment. XELLENT now has its crystal clear purity and 96% alcohol content.

Glacier water / Following a rest period of several months, the distillate is now very gently and gradually reduced – with further short rest periods in between – with the pure glacier water from Mount Titlis to an alcohol content of 40%. XELLENT has attained its status as a Premium Vodka through a multi-stage filtration process. The distinguished distillate is then poured into the distinctive red XELLENT bottle and exported all around the world.

FROM VODKA TO GIN

The already enjoyable Ultra Premium XELLENT Swiss Vodka is also used as a basis for the XELLENT Swiss Edelweiss Gin. This exquisite combination gives the gin a quite extraordinary suppleness. The Master Distiller selects the various herbs for the gin according to the most stringent criteria. In addition to the juniper berries, carefully cultivated edelweiss flowers, freshly picked lemon balm and elderflowers from the region are selected, in addition to the woodruff collected in the forest and 20 other herbs. After the harvest, the herbs are carefully dried to preserve their flower and their essential oils. The flowers and leaves are mixed with fresh herbs and added to the vodka. They give the gin a special extra element, in addition to the typical juniper taste. After a fourth, gentle distillation and a re-reduction of the alcohol content using Titlis glacier water, the XELLENT Swiss Edelweiss Gin is now ready for enjoyment.

XELLENT :
PURE SWISSNESS

The way XELLENT products are made, down to the very last drop, is grounded in the notion of "Swissness". In keeping with the traditional craft, the raw materials are sourced from the breathtaking landscapes of Switzerland. The natural ingredients are obtained mostly in central Switzerland and both their production and their processing take place in an cultural landscape that is unparalleled. The Master Distiller – a genuine expert in his field – takes personal charge of the company's own garden and the surrounding countryside to grow and harvest certain plants. The company's passion for tradition and outstanding value goes hand-in-hand with a capacity for innovation and state-of-the-art techniques.

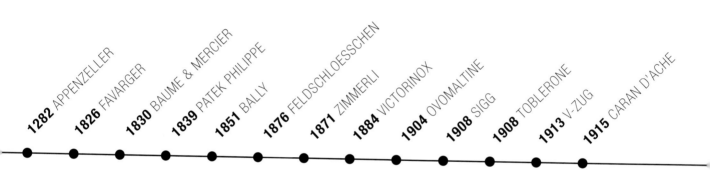

1282 APPENZELLER 1826 FAVARGER 1830 BAUME & MERCIER 1839 PATEK PHILIPPE 1851 BALLY 1876 FELDSCHLOESSCHEN 1871 ZIMMERLI 1884 VICTORINOX 1904 OVOMALTINE 1908 SIGG 1908 TOBLERONE 1913 V-ZUG 1915 CARAN D'ACHE

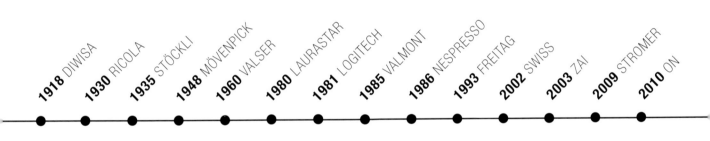

1918 DIWISA 1930 RICOLA 1935 STÖCKLI 1948 MÖVENPICK 1960 VALSER 1980 LAURASTAR 1981 LOGITECH 1985 VALMONT 1986 NESPRESSO 1993 FREITAG 2002 SWISS 2003 ZAI 2009 STROMER 2010 ON

Websites

APPENZELLER.CH

BALLY.COM

BAUME-ET-MERCIER.COM

CARANDACHE.COM

FAVARGER.COM

FELDSCHLOESSCHEN.COM

FREITAG.COM

LAURASTAR.COM

LOGITECH.COM

MOEVENPICK-ICECREAM.COM

NESPRESSO.COM

ON-RUNNING.COM

OVOMALTINE.CH

PATEK.COM

RICOLA.COM

SIGG.COM

STOECKLI.CH

STROMERBIKE.COM

SWISS.COM

TOBLERONE.COM

VZUG.COM

EVALMONT.COM

VALSER.CH

VICTORINOX.COM

XELLENT.CH

ZIMMERLI.COM

ZAI.CH

PHOTO CREDITS

ACKNOWLEDGEMENTS

Carl Elsener, Claudia Mader, Sophie Aliot-Siret, Sophie Vann Guillon, Didier Guillon, Yoann Sevin, Helena Meier, Elisabeth Mild, Madeleine Hügli, Monika Walser, Sonja Ptassek, Alain Zimmermann, Stéphanie Joire, Nicole Boghossian, Valérie Epinay, Gabriela Gerber, Astrid Herrmann, Lena Fisler, Laura Scorza, Cédric Focking-Schneider, Barbara Sutter, Colas Dupont, Yael Kusch, Linda Hufschmid, Sonja Baumann, Sam Tinson, Jan-Philip Seger, Linda Hufschmid, Hans Meier, Elisabeth Janschitz, Sven Ziörjen, Anja Schmidt-Amelung, Marco Alessandri, Philipp Häseli, Philipp Hofmann, Vesna Stimac, Claudia Hollstein, Antoine & Frédérique, Vicky Weiler, Jean-Luc Palleja, Charles Stoyanov, Régis Bouaziz, Gérard Wegener, François Mironnet, Alcidia Moucheboeuf, Eduardo De Barros, Pierre-Yves Chomarat, Tiffany Büsser, Clémence de Laubier, Jérôme Favoulet, Virginie Gilbert, Haifa, Flor Amores, Cécile Benoist, Gaëlle Silasi.

Editorial concept & production / LBC sarl (Geneve)
Director of Publication / Jean-Philippe Zérafa
Chief Editor / Tiffany Büsser
Design / Clémence de Laubier
Translations / Datawords
Website / www.lbcvmg.com

IMPRINT

This volume was completed to print on printing presses ATAR Roto Presse
in 2014 in Geneva (Switzerland).